The Touching Place

Steve Butler

The Touching Place

The whole body participation of

the worshipping community

As submitted to the University of Edinburgh

MTh by Research, Sept 2005

Sermon in stone

The other day, I noticed an elderly man struggling to dislodge a huge stone from the coping of our churchyard wall. Eventually, he succeeded in shifting it. I watched him stagger up the steps of the porch, and, with a huge effort, hurl it at the locked door of our church. Then he stumbled away before I could catch him.

Back at the Rectory, I told the family what I'd seen. We wondered who this poor chap was, and what was his problem. Was he perhaps in poor mental health? Was he drunk? Was he both? I ventured an alternative hypothesis. I suggested that he was probably a retired clergyman and of entirely sound and sober mind. I surmised that he had served faithfully in a series of benefices, each one blessed by a splendid church building for which he had been responsible. I speculated further that each of these proud buildings had proved inimical to the mission he had believed himself called to fulfil. I suggested that the burden of these buildings had at last broken his spirit. Now, several times a week, he was taking the train up from the College of St Barnabas, Lingfield, and was picking off the churches of his former diocese one by one.

Before each great door, like a latter-day Ezekiel, he was performing an act of "prophetic symbolism", invoking the judgement of the Lord on a community that, though called to live in tents, had preferred to build itself temples. Merry laughter rang round the Rectory. They thought I was joking.

John Pridmore, Rector of Hackney; The Church Times, 3rd December 2004

Contents

Chapter One

Christian Sacred Place: a background and agenda for the worshipping community

Chapter Two

Embodiment: a rationale for the importance of the body in environments for worship and liturgical practice.

Chapter Three

Seeing is believing

Chapter Four

Auditory experience in the worship environment. The physical and psychophysical effects of sound and of making music.

Chapter Five

Touching the void – being present to ritual event and re-membering the body

Chapter One

Christian Sacred Place: a background and agenda for the worshipping community

Introduction - a building-formed community?

In the period leading up to this project, it was my task to create a website that represented and served my own local church community. With no previous experience of the genre or skills required, it occurred to me that a visit to a broad cross-section of existing church websites might usefully inform my choices and preferences. The great majority of the sites I visited included on their home page a photograph or drawing of a church building. Many offered virtual tours of the building and its associated amenities. Some sites offered news of renovation and development schemes (with associated appeals for funding), together with written and photographic records of the building's history. To an impartial observer, a reasonable assumption would be that the contemporary Christian church in the United Kingdom is a property-related institution, with considerable interests and resources committed to a national network of heritable heritage.

The institutional church, it may be argued, unintentionally or intentionally thinks of itself principally as the occupier and maintainer of edifices that redeem the landscape (urban and rural) and which symbolise upon it (by means of well 'branded' architectural styling) the timeless moral and spiritual bulwark that stands between a changing world and the eternal realm. Culturally, this may be the background to the contemporary prioritisation of public heritage funding for the restoration of those traditional church buildings deemed to be of architectural significance. If we imagine an audit of shared cultural assumptions, it is easy to suppose that in any random sample of people presented with the verbal cue *'church'*, most would contrive a mental picture of a stone building replete with spire. This image is, of course, an idealised invention that locates the church safely in the unthreatening role of a monument to an institution of the past. In Harold Turner's description of the surprising influence of the nineteenth-century Gothic revival in English church architecture, he notes that assumptions about deep-rooted tradition can be misplaced:

> The consequence.... is quite clear – the standard Anglican parish church as we have known it over the past century, especially in the towns, with its cruciform shape, deep chancel for a surpliced choir, railed sanctuary at the far end, covered altar with candlesticks and a cross, rather inconspicuous side pulpit, litany desks, and prominent brass eagle lectern. It is difficult to realise what a novelty much of this was until a mere one hundred and forty years ago.[1]

My proposition is that at the start of this third Christian millennium, the institutional churches (at least in the West), in the midst of long-term numerical and cultural decline, are taking little interest in the problem of having become a predominantly 'building-formed community', at the expense of being a 'story-formed community'. If we accept that the visible church must physically 'be' somewhere, then my initial intention in this project will be to explore the constituent criteria for place as the worshipping community should understand it. Subsequently, in the light of some enquiry

---

1 Harold Turner, <u>From Temple To Meeting House: the phenomenology and theology of places of worship</u> (The Hague: Mouton, 1979), p.249.

into the architectural and environmental-psychological perspectives on private and public space, I will make some proposals as to how these perspectives might inform any ecclesiology that envisions the use and creation of contemporary places for worship.

Initially it will be necessary to trace the worshipping community's relationship with designated worship space. Why is it that the church has come to be so closely associated with its architectural manifestation? What is the nature of the quest for sacred place, and how has the church responded through the long-term processes of institutional evolution, within the continuum of historical context, cultural change and theological understanding?

Place and sanctity

The human experience of place is of philosophical and anthropological interest as well as being central to Christian theology. To be a person is 'to be there', in a particular place. Physical place is the scaffold upon which the individual and the community construct their own realities. It does not possess an objectivity of its own, but may be understood as a container for the rituals and symbols by which we interpret the world and evolve necessary cultures and societal codes. Philip Sheldrake's work on sacred space is grounded in the idea that the contemporary context of globalisation and plurality creates a new significance for the role of place in Western society[2]. If, in the past, most people's worlds extended as far as the parish boundary, the experience of life with global reach challenges the comfortable

2 Philip Sheldrake, Spaces for the Sacred: place, memory and identity (London: SCM, 2001).

notion of place in the process of defining the self. Thrown back on itself in the search for meaning, the self faces alienation from the sense of 'the local' or 'home'. For Sheldrake this explains the preoccupation in the West with the search for roots, and the converse fear of rootlessness. The origins of this sense of loss of home may be traced to the development of industrialisation and urbanisation, and where globalisation creates the enhanced possibility of culture that is no longer specific to place. Where cultures are no longer homogeneous and may be plural or fragmented, there is the potential for the deepening alienation that the sociologist Peter Berger called "metaphysical homelessness"[3].

Religious anthropologists also identify the need for a sense of home in their definition of place that is sacred. According to Eliade[4], certain places and structures appeal to a "nostalgia for paradise", which is an expression of a thirst to transcend the human condition. Gerardus van der Leeuw[5] describes the element of home in terms of a place of comfort and familiarity, "where the heart of the world could be approached". For Sheldrake, all individuals need a sense of place that provides access to the sacred and thereby to life itself. In the ancient world, say the anthropologists, there was a clearer distinction between sacred and non-sacred place. Sacred place was a place of regeneration, creativity and transformation, which provided some kind of stability in the midst of a chaotic world. Turner provides a fourfold summary of sacred place as defined by the phenomenology of religion[6]:

---

3 Peter Berger, The Homeless Mind : modernization and consciousness (Hammondsworth: Penguin, 1974).

4 Mircea Eliade, Patterns in Comparative Religion (London: Sheed and Ward, 1958), p.383.

5 Gerardus van der Leeuw, Religion in Essence and Manifestation: a study in phenomenology, trans. J.E.Turner, 2 vols (Glos, Mass.: Peter Smith, 1967), p.2:401.

6 This is a summary of Turner, From Temple To Meeting House, pp.8-20.

Centre – sacred place is where human experience finds order amid the uncertainties, and where the orderliness of the heavenly world is somehow reflected or represented on earth.

Meeting Point – places becomes sacred where the gods somehow come to connect with their creatures, at the site of communication between two worlds. This will typically involve threshold rituals at the boundary between the two, and mountain typeology.

Microcosm – places where the qualities of the divine life are made present in the earthly experience, and which must therefore be made suitable – a replica prototype of the heavenly realm, incorporating as far as possible the appropriate sacred geometry.

Transcendent-Immanent Presence – sacred places house the divine presence with a degree of guarantee, even though the divine beings, by their nature, transcend such places.

Recognising that the Christian understanding of sacred place needs to be set in the context of distinctive faith traditions, Turner's argument is that within the semitic religions, two types of sacred place have emerged; the *temple* type (domus dei) and the *meeting house* type (domus ecclesiae). In a review of the historical development of Christian worship places Turner seeks to demonstrate that despite the dominance of the former[7], the latter is the authentic norm in theological terms.

---

7 "While the essentials of sacred place do not include any edifice, the most characteristic form of its fullest development is found in the temple complex of buildings". Ibid.p.34.

My intention here is to use Turner's model and suggest that the historical diversion of the Christian experiment has been to invest in static architectural forms.

The temple procession

In the patriarchal narratives, the earliest material concerning revelation in the history of the nomadic Hebrews (and most clearly in the Exodus material concerning Moses and the revealing of the Hebraic code) it may be argued that a core concept is that of sanctity and sanctuary in the midst of unknown places. Meaning became associated with places that were identified with divine encounters, which correspond with Turner's phenomenological criteria. Shrines were created to mark out sites connected with significant historical events. Most importantly, however, there is in the divine revelation a directive that this activity should not be limited by time and space. In other words, the idea of sanctuary is not one of a holy, static place. What distinguishes the nomadic Hebrew people from other contemporary religious systems is that they are to be liberated from any kind of dependence on location. Thus, instead of the people travelling to or with God, God covenants to travel with the people. The altar is to be made moveable (Exodus 17: 4-6)[8]: "Let them make a sanctuary, that I may dwell in their midst" (Exodus 25:8). The details provided for the making of the Ark of the Covenant (Exodus 25:10-22) are clear in their demands that it must be portable. Wherever it stands, a tent is to be erected over it to signify the presence of God among his people. If location is to be sacred, if worship is to

---

8 All biblical quotations are taken from the NRSV.

be offered somewhere, then the principle is that the divine encounter is not to be pinned down.

From this starting point, the story of ancient Judaism can be characterised in the drift towards the location of sacred worship in the Jerusalem temple, and ultimately away again in the diaspora of the synagogue movement. The story of the Jerusalem temple is arguably a metaphor for the ebb and flow of the Jewish cult's successes and failures in understanding its status and calling. Essentially, the creation of the temple during the monarchy period (despite the pained warnings of the prophets) located the Ark in a permanent and protected place of grandeur, a site which in its scale reflected the political ambitions and power of the nation state. In Giles' words, "The Jewish religion thereby was nationalised, centralised and politicised; it became static"[9].

The destruction of the temple in 587BC, its subsequent rebuilding and ultimate destruction again in AD70, provide the background to the dramatic story of the survival and reinvention of Judaism which eventually dispensed with sanctuary and sacrifice, located worship in the home and the synagogue (understood to mean gathering), and provided a model for the emerging Christian church. This model recovered the idea that worship could be located anywhere, and that there was no need for a priestly class.

Just as the revelation of God dwelling in the midst of his people had been a foundational concept at the emergence of the Jewish religion, the Christian faith emerged with a clear understanding of temple and sanctuary as metaphors of Christ present in the body of the faithful. Jesus himself in his earthly ministry had turned his back on the household and chosen a lifestyle

9 Richard Giles, <u>Re-Pitching The Tent</u> (Norwich: Canterbury Press, 1996), p.25.

of itinerant travelling and displacement. The itinerant character of the subsequent worshipping community can be seen to begin with the empty tomb beyond which the presence or place of Christ was no longer to be specifically embodied. The writer to the Hebrews comprehensively reinterprets the concepts of temple, sacrifice and priesthood in terms of Jesus' own ministry and sacrificial death:

> ...in the new Christian dispensation, there is no longer any need for sanctuary, altar, sacrifice or human priesthood, nor for a temple to house them. All of these have been rendered obsolete by the role of Jesus, the exalted one, and the concept of temple transposed from dead to living stones. Our home is "the greater and more perfect tent not made with hands, that is, not of this creation". (Hebrews 9:11).[10]

In *The Acts of the Apostles*, the metaphor of being 'on the way' becomes a definition of the faith as revelation becomes focused not on a place or a land, but on a person. The early church was concerned to explore the reality of the 'new temple' that is the relationship between God, Jesus and the Christian community: "...we are a temple of the living God, just as God said, "I will live in them and move among them"." (1 Corinthians 5:9). The church in the New Testament is never understood to be a place or a building, but always the community where Christ is with his people: not a sacred place, but a sacred people. The Belgian liturgist Frederic Debuyst characterises the earliest Christian worship as a "reactualisation"[11] of the death and resurrection of Christ which makes the place of worship a "paschal meeting room"[12]:

---

10 Ibid, p.49.

11 Frederic Debuyst, <u>Modern Architecture and Christian Celebration </u>(London: Lutterworth, 1968), p.18.

12 Ibid. p.18.

In the early liturgy, the worshipper's attention was not directed to objects (for instance, to the altar). It was entirely concentrated on the anamnesis itself... the essential thing, in these early days, was to obey the Lord's command to gather together.... first of all to celebrate his ever active presence in their midst (communion) and to transmit the power of this presence to the world (mission).[13]

If there was no initial interest in the first Christian centuries for the building of sanctuaries, then Turner argues that this was not simply expediency on the part of the suppressed house church, but the normative expression of the new faith's priorities. The third century saw the first pilgrimages to the Holy Land and this activity expanded as Constantine built shrines at important historical sites associated with Jesus, saints and martyrs. This was the first evidence of the drift back to the notion that sanctity belonged in physical objects and places.

The fourth century saw critical developments in the achievement of state legitimisation for the church, which brought with it the need for public architecture. In centuries which followed, the story of the church included the slow evolution from the communal house church with no specific associated architecture, to the Roman-inspired basilica, and then through the Romanesque, Byzantine, Gothic, Renaissance and Baroque architectural eras. Of particular interest to Turner[14] are the liturgical emphases enshrined in the church-building which followed the Reformation and the Gothic revival of the nineteenth century, as he traces the church's instinct for the *domus dei*. This he argues is present even in the architecture of the Reformation which heralded the community of worship; the restoration of the sacrament to the

13 Debuyst, <u>Modern Architecture and Christian Celebration</u>, p.20.

14 Turner, <u>From Temple To Meeting House</u>, p.205ff.

laity; the repositioning of the Lord's table in the midst of the people; the reuniting of word and sacrament; and the abandoning of interior subdivisions. Despite this he demonstrates the reformers' tendency to use the word 'temple' to imply a continuity with the Jerusalem temple, imbuing the building with derived holiness.

The Protestant church building programmes of the seventeenth and eighteenth centuries produced many examples of innovative meeting house shapes (the 'protestant plain style') and the emergence of the auditorium model, whereby the preaching of the Word could be heard by as many people as was practically possible. Even these traditions did not escape the far-reaching influence of the nineteenth-century Gothic revival, with the widespread re-establishment of separate sanctuaries, and the attempt to create a sense of awe and mystery using the finest materials and elaborate ornamentation.

This history, says Debuyst, is "of an evolution from the primitive memorial – the anamnesis – to the external stone monument"[15]. Writing in the 1960's, Debuyst reflects the spirit of the twentieth-century Liturgical Movement in identifying a new hunger for a move away from the dead monument to the living memorial. Emerging throughout the twentieth century but bearing fruit at Vatican II and beyond, the Liturgical Movement was a cross-denominational response to rapid theological discovery and societal change. In essence, it embodied a move away from excessive individualisation, and the recovery of a more corporate vision of less hierarchical and frequent eucharistic worship, in the spirit of primitive Christianity. In Giles' words:

---

15 Ibid, p.29.

20

"We no longer gather merely to gaze at Christ, the image of God; in the renewed liturgical assembly we enter into the mystery of becoming Christ."[16]

And yet, despite thirty years of reflection on the implications for liturgical space, the institutional churches have been slow to respond. A quick look through recent editions of the architectural journal Church Building Magazine[17] suggests that worshipping communities understand their physical manifestation in terms of buildings that give the church a significant place on the landscape. Here, the architect's role is to create or reshape a material, external prominence, whilst retaining many of the familiar interior arrangements. For Turner, contemporary church-building still exhibits confusion about whether to express numinosity (typically streamlined verticality) or community (functional architecture which stresses the life of the congregation). For many mainstream worshipping communities there is a constant theme of struggle to fund the restoration of existing buildings whose exterior and interior arrangements will continue to enshrine a *domus dei* model. It is as though the inexorable appeal of finding the sacred in material places, particularly in designated buildings, is an instinct that the worshipping community finds irresistible.

The monumental problem

We have already seen that there are historic and universal models of sacred place. If these patterns are identifiable across religious systems and cultural epochs, then the conclusion can be drawn that the Christian community will

16 Giles, Re-Pitching The Tent, p.83.

17 Church Building Magazine (Manchester: Gabriel Communications)

inevitably conform to these patterns irrespective of its theology. Turner's description and analysis of the principal *domus dei* and *domus ecclesiae* forms are in themselves extremely useful distinctions, but what Turner has failed to address is that there may, by definition, be no meaningful separation of the two.

De-emphasis of church buildings has always been associated with expressions of radical Christianity, notably in the earliest Christian communities, in some examples of the sixteenth-century Reformation, and currently in the context of rapid church-growth movements in the charismatic, evangelical traditions in both Western and non-Western contexts. The tension arises from the inescapable practicality that any continuing worshipping community with particular liturgical activities will ultimately recognise a need for suitable accommodation for its purpose. Thus, even if the community in question has a well developed sense of the locus of sanctity residing in the body of the faithful, the spiritual life of the community must have a physical and historical embodiment. Any holiness derived from the personalised temple of 'Jesus-in-community' will inevitably become associated with the place of worship, and where the community locates itself for anything longer than a short stay, the historical significance of the ongoing experience of divine saving activity (i.e. the weekly eucharist, rites of passage, annual festivals) will imbue the designated place with cumulative sacred meaning.

An architectural perspective may help us to see that neither the physical place nor the worshipping community are the locus of the sanctity, but that the meaning of place as sacred is to be found in the relationship between the two.

The ritual-architectural event

> A building standing empty is not a whole building. It is only a beginning. We cannot understand it until we fill it with people, if only in our imaginations.[18]

In his recent and comprehensive work on the hermeneutics of sacred architecture, Lindsay Jones argues that sanctity of space is not to be understood as an objective condition, but is derived from specific interaction between people and architectural constructs. It is, therefore, a relational concept associated with located ritual events. What is important, says Jones, are not monuments but monumental occasions based on largely unconscious processes of interpretation which constitute a hermeneutic of sacred architecture. Sacred architecture is therefore to be understood in terms of the events that create interaction between buildings and people:

> From this hermeneutical frame, it is not the buildings but the human experience or apprehension of buildings that holds our attention....From this perspective, the locus of meaning resides neither in the building itself (a physical object) nor in the mind of the beholder (a human subject), but rather in the negotiation or the interactive relation that subsumes both building and beholder in the *ritual-architectural event* in which buildings and human participants alike are involved.[19]

This is an understanding of sacred architecture in terms of situational events, rather than what might be presumed to be 'real', objective or static meanings.

18 Anita Abramovitz, cited in Lindsay Jones, The Hermeneutics of Sacred Architecture, Volume 1 (Cambridge MA: Harvard University Press, 2000), p.38.

19 Ibid, p.41.

From this perspective we may understand that although the world is full of ancient monuments of religious significance, there is generally a limited appreciation of the rituals and ceremonials that were associated with the creation of such places, or indeed of the dynamics that invoked critical religious experiences for the communities that used them in the intervening generations. These dynamics, relational as they are, located in time and in the specifics of prevailing culture, are, by definition, ephemeral. Problematically, this means that spaces understood to be sacred are often trading on the significance of ritual events that have become detached from their original historical and cultural context. This scenario, which might commonly characterise the experience of a typical institutional church community, provides some explanation for the dissonance between the theology of the *domus ecclesiae* and the experience of the *domus dei*.

Jones' task is to examine the nature of what he calls the "quality of allurement"[20] that causes individuals and communities to interpret some architectures as sacred. The mistake, in Jones' terms, is to think of the community and its worship space separately, whereby the participants are merely observers or consumers of the architectural arrangements and their ritual associations. Instead, place and community are to be imagined as being in an interactive conversation or game:

> ....first, the stone, wood and iron of the buildings themselves, which together are imagined as one 'player' in the hermeneutical game; second, human beings, heavily burdened with expectations, traditions and religious opinions, imagined somewhat more easily as additional players; and third, the ceremonial occasion as the activity

---

20 Ibid, p.74ff.

24

or game (or conversation) which actually brings buildings and people into a to-and-fro involvement with one another.[21]

With this model in mind, we may rightly begin to enquire as to the efficiency and efficacy of a place of worship as a conduit of this elaborate interaction. Why might it be that some games are clearly engaging and fun, when others are tedious? Why is one conversation clearly imaginative and an exchange of heartfelt empathy, when another is self-centred and dull? In architectural terms, why is it that some spaces can be ignored or be neutral, when others inspire fascination and demand a committed response? For Jones, the agenda is about further understanding the "interactive relation that subsumes both building and beholder".[22]

The empty space

The British theatrical producer and director, Peter Brook, famously described the "theatre of the invisible-made-visible" in the 1960s, and the power in the idea of the stage being a place where the invisible can appear[23]. Apart from having a distinctly incarnational ring, the theatrical dynamic accords well with the theological emphasis, described above, of worship places being characterised as transient or itinerant. If the worshipping community is to respond at all to the theological norm of God promising to be in the midst of his people, who are constantly on the move, then the idea of demolishing and rebuilding traditional buildings, or of constantly finding temporary spaces to rent, is problematic. However, if the model of ritual-architectural

21 Ibid, p.49.

22 Ibid, p.41.

23 Peter Brook, The Empty Space (London: Penguin, 1968), p.47.

event is adopted, then the life of the worshipping community is transient *by definition*. Thus, it is not necessarily, or exclusively, the form of architectural arrangements that needs to be understood, but the spatial arrangements and ceremonials on an event-by-event basis. This would seem to direct attention to the study of spatial interiors as the critical locus:

> Religious architecture then, epitomises in a particularly strong fashion the irony.... that the greatest significance and utility in construction, whether of moulded clay vessels or of grand cathedrals, often lies not in the solid masses themselves but in the hollowness they create, in the spaces, contexts, ambiences, and significant voids that come into being via the processes of construction[24].

Herman Hertzberger, a leading post-war Dutch architectural theorist, argues that constructive design for people generally should be flexible and polyvalent. The doctrine behind his position is that mono-functional design is proscriptive, and contributes to a uniformity that is oppressive. Increasingly homogeneous forms (witness most housing and retail developments) diminish the variations that allow for individual identity. Hertzberger calls for design that offers incentives to users to influence the space in a way which will enhance and affirm their identity, because the central concern is the way in which the architectural form and its users interact. Akin to Jones' "conversation", Hertzberger likens the interaction to the effects of written words and sentences, whose impact depends on how they are read. In this way architectural forms should permit interpretation and take on identity through being used.

---

24 Jones, <u>The Hermeneutics of Sacred Architecture</u>, Volume 2, p.185.

For the worshipping community this holds the promise of forms that are transient and dynamically related to its ongoing life:

> What we make must constitute an offer; it must have the capacity to elicit, time and again, specific reactions befitting specific situations; so it must not be merely neutral and flexible – and hence non-specific – but it must possess that wider efficaciousness that we call polyvalence.[25]

Importantly, from the architectural perspective represented by Jones and Hertzberger, the creation of efficacious spaces must include the possibility of people being able to participate in the making of the space they occupy. Here, the more that individuals and communities are able to project something of their own identity onto the forms they inhabit, the greater the possibility of a dialogue whereby users will experience ways in which the environment will colour, inform and complete their own existence. The proposal in this project is that this dynamic should be a requisite part of the worshipping community's use of space.

One of the practical categories of sacred architectural 'allurement' identified by Jones is 'theatrical'. This refers to design strategies in the context of stationary stage and audience scenarios, which are conceived to do everything possible to encourage the participation of reluctant spectators. As a simple example of such a strategy, Jones refers to the work of Peter Hammond (a late contributor to the Liturgical Movement), to his core principle of Christian worship as a principally corporate activity, and to his related endorsement of contemporary developments in the use of circular or

---

25 Herman Hertzberger, <u>Lessons for Students in Architecture</u> (Amsterdam: Uitgeverij, 1991), p.150.

elliptical church plans that create the environment for communal participation in the proceedings[26]. In the same way, Jones describes moveable seating and the dynamic options it provides, as a most basic example of theatrical, ritual-architectural allurement that involves the potential participation of people physically, rather than only intellectually. The nature of this physical or embodied participation will be explored in the following chapters.

Conclusion

I have argued that despite the weight of biblical emphasis on sacred place as a dynamic phenomenon, associated with the presence and activity of the worshipping community (as espoused by successive radicals including the Reformers and the twentieth century Liturgical Movement) the Western church has consistently been unable to resist monument-centred priorities (Turner's *domus dei*). History would appear to demonstrate that it is unrealistic to appeal entirely to an alternative *domus ecclesiae* model (community-centred) as each continuing worshipping community attends to the inevitable need for suitable accommodation. There is, therefore, for many institutional worshipping communities a dissonance in their practice (between the theology of the *domus ecclesiae* and the experience of *domus dei*) that may in part explain common experiences of difficulty and diminishment.

Although Turner's classifications are useful, I have suggested that it is the polarisation of the two that is problematic. Taking inspiration from the

---

26 Peter Hammond (ed.), <u>Towards a Church Architecture</u> (London: Architectural Press, 1962).

architectural theorists, Jones and Hertzberger, I have argued that neither the physical place nor the worshipping community are the locus of sanctity, but that the meaning of space as sacred is to be found in the relationship between the two. This is an understanding of sacred form in terms of relational and located events, rather than what might be presumed to be real, objective or static meanings. As Jones puts it, place and community are to be understood as participants in an interactive negotiation or conversation – a dynamic process that is, by definition, ephemeral.

In his rejection of the "dead monument" in favour of the "living memorial"[27] of the Paschal meeting room, Debuyst describes the need for a "real interior"[28] which expresses a fundamental hospitality in the place of celebration. Although he appeals, appropriately, for worship spaces that "above all, enable a deeply human contact to be nurtured"[29], Debuyst exhibits (in common with other writers reviewed here) somewhat superficial remedies. I would suggest that further exploration is required into the nature of the interaction of forms and users if the sanctity of contemporary worship space is to be understood. If we accept the principle that spaces and their occupants are transformed on each occasion of their dynamic interaction (a model that sits comfortably with the theological model of sacred place outlined earlier) then the task here will be an exploration of the nature of these potential transformations.

27 Debuyst, Modern Architecture and Christian Celebration, p.29.

28 Ibid, p.30.

29 Ibid, p.59.

Chapter Two

Embodiment: a rationale for the importance of the body in environments for worship and liturgical practice.

Introduction

In its ritual events, the physically-gathered community's encounter with the divine is characterised by its interaction with the specific locale in which it finds itself. By implication, the quest for appropriate worship patterns must include an acknowledgement that physically-located, bodily experience is the basis of any such interaction. In order to interact with place and ritual event, the community processes the vast range of sensory information that is immediately available. If the visual, aural, olfactory and physical receptors are the principal paths to the interaction that informs the present worship experience (and to which the individuals who make up the community bring their previous accumulated knowledge and experience) then a theology of embodiment is required to underpin further thinking about how the community might participate in the making of the spaces it occupies.

In arguing that contemporary worship practice should prioritise the principle of embodiment, I will explore the development (and predominant problem) of the idea of the body in Christian thought, with particular reference to the influence of the Reformation; the related cultural revolution brought about by aspects of the Enlightenment; the written and printed word; and the prevailing dominance of visual culture. In identifying these developments as the source of the disembodiment of Western (and particularly Reformed) worship, I will argue that 'body theology' (with particular reference to the work of James Nelson) as well as aspects of feminist theology should inform an understanding of worship as whole-body experience. In so doing I will draw attention to examples of embodied spirituality throughout Christian history that would support a re-emphasis of the body for the worshipping community.

In conclusion, I will appeal to the work of Charles Davis who argues that the only authentic human responses (spiritual responses) are those that are *affective*. This differs from the detached observation, assessment or judgement we could call 'intellectual', and which is the lingering, but withering, inheritance of the long history of theological dualism. Where Davis suggests that authentic spirituality is nurtured in experience that has been conceived not in the brain, but in the whole body, I will argue that worship practice should embrace rather than fear such affectivity, and set an agenda reminiscent of Lindsay Jones' qualities of allurement for the use of designated spaces for worship.

One is the Body

> "It is still true that the Deity gives us, according to His promise, not His thoughts or His convictions but His flesh and blood.... We only believe in those thoughts which have been conceived not in the brain but in the whole body." *W.B. Yeats*[30]

---

30 W.B.Yeats, from his introduction to: Fenollosa, Ernest Francisco and Ezra Pound. <u>Certain Noble Plays of Japan:</u> from the Manuscripts of Ernest Fenollosa, chosen and finished by Ezra Pound (Dundrum: Cuala Press, 1916), p.xviii.

"Soul and body, body and soul - how mysterious they were! There was animalism in the soul, and the body had its moments of spirituality. The senses could refine, and the intellect could degrade. Who could say where the fleshly impulse ceased, or the physical impulse began? *Oscar Wilde[31]*

Human activities associated with worship are, like every other human activity, made up of highly complex responses, both conscious and unconscious, to a vast range of stimuli that combine sensory input with learned experience. We assimilate the wisdom of the past, says Walter Ong, by learning how to organise the "sensorium, the entire sensory apparatus as an operational complex"[32].

Obvious as this perspective may seem, it appears to be absent from much ecclesiological and liturgical discussion in a cultural context where belief and ideology have been dominated by the Enlightenment belief that the mind must take precedence over the body. On the other hand everyday experience and the human sciences tell us that the mind and body are a unity. The elaborate judgements and instinctive adjustments made by the athlete, or by the visual or performance artist, can only reach the highest level when mind and body fully synchronise. Most of us use gestural language and an array of complicated body language as we interact with others. Indeed, the thought processes, responses and feelings of deaf people are articulated through sign language. Our voices carry impressive ranges of tone and linguistic inflexion as we communicate nuanced reactions. The intricate control of complex facial muscles is revealingly connected to our deepest motivations, helping to

---

31 Oscar Wilde, The Picture of Dorian Gray. In: The complete plays, stories, poems, and novels (Bombay: Wilco International, 1963), 17-167, 56.

32 Walter Ong, The Presence of the Word (New Haven: Yale University Press, 1967), p.6.

establish social contact by enabling our prediction of the motivations of others. Children first learn to count using their hands and fingers. We recognise this to be a natural learning mode, and educationalists espouse 'hands-on' methods of understanding, recognising that mechanical skills are the basis of cognitive development and indeed the development of technology and of civilisations. For R.D. Laing "we live equally out of our bodies and out of our minds"[33], to such a degree that psychosis is to be understood as a loss of the continuity of body and mind:

> The embodied person has a sense of being flesh and blood and bones, of being biologically alive and real: he knows himself to be substantial. To the extent that he is thoroughly 'in' his body, he is likely to have a sense of personal continuity in time. He will experience himself as subject to the dangers that threaten his body, the dangers of attack, mutilation, disease, decay, and death. He is implicated in bodily desire, and the gratifications and frustrations of the body. The individual thus has as his starting-point an experience of his body as a base from which he can be a person with other human beings.[34]

We know that our relationality depends on visible and tangible bodies that make themselves known and sensible to one other. With the body we place ourselves in the world of experience, and embodiment may therefore be described as the true nature of experience. What we desire, believe and feel is both accumulated and articulated through bodily activity, which may be said to constitute our very personalities and expressions of self. Nicholas

---

33 Ronald D. Laing, The Politics of Experience (New York: Pantheon Books, 1967), p. 59.
34 Ronald D. Laing, The Divided Self (Harmondsworth/Penguin, 1965), p.67.

Humphrey, in his 'History of the Mind', lists how consciousness itself is to be defined as a function of the sensory being:

1. To be conscious is essentially to have sensations: that is, to have affect-laden mental representations of something happening here and now to me.

2. The subject of consciousness, 'I', is an embodied self. In the absence of bodily sensations 'I' would cease. Sentio, ergo sum - I feel, therefore I am.

3. All sensations are implicitly located at the spatial boundary between me and not-me, and at the temporal boundary between past and future: that is, in the 'present'.

4. For human beings, most sensations occur in the province of one of the five senses (sight, sound, touch, smell, taste). Hence most human states of consciousness have one or other of these qualities. There are no non-sensory, amodal conscious states.

5. Mental activities other than those involving direct sensation enter consciousness only in so far as they are accompanied by 'reminders' of sensation, such as happens in the case of mental imagery and dreams.

6. This is no less true of conscious thoughts, ideas, beliefs... Conscious thoughts are typically 'heard' as images of voices in the head - and without this sensory component they would drop away.

7. If and when we claim that another living organism is conscious we are implying that it too is the subject of sensations (although not necessarily of a kind we are familiar with).

8. If we were to claim that a non-living organism was conscious, the same would have to apply. A mechanical robot for example would

not be conscious unless it were specifically designed to have sensation as well as perception (whatever the design involved).[35]

And yet it is common for us to regard the self, our inmost essence, as something incorporeal, an immaterial phantom that is ultimately independent of the body. As Sarah Coakley says in the introduction to her collection of essays on religion and the body, despite a "legion of cries" in social theory for a greater sense of self as body, "the spectres of religious and philosophical dualism die hard"[36]. Contemporary "mainstream" Christian worship (and most certainly the conservative, kerygmatic culture of my own Presbyterian upbringing) would appear to be governed by a prevailing assumption that the flesh is an obstacle to the freeing of the spirit, a theological dualism with a long heritage and a tenacious grip.

Two is the person

Early Christianity emerged in the context of a civilisation which, in the centuries immediately before and after its arrival, was inextricably shaped by Hellenism. At the heart of this was the Platonic relegation of the material world to a pale shadow or simulation of eternal and pure ideas, which exist in a non-sensorial world, beyond what is apparent. For Plato the destiny of the soul was to ascend from the body and merge into the godhead. This depended on a 'seeing' beyond the material world, enabling the true philosopher's quest for a freeing and separation of the soul from the body. The most important theme of his famous cave allegory is the belief that there

---

35 Nicholas Humphrey, A History of the Mind (London: Chatto & Windus, 1992), pp.97-98.

36 Sarah Coakley, Religion and the Body (Cambridge: Cambridge University Press, 1997), introduction.

are invisible truths lying under the apparent surface of things, which only the most enlightened person can grasp. This fundamental concept became the basis of subsequent gnostic systems (a variety of dualistic movements following a path of asceticism, characterised by rejection of matter and body, sexuality and male-female relationships) and influenced the new Christian movement to a remarkable degree, given its more holistic Hebraic origins where there was a unity of body and soul, and of flesh animated by soul[37].

Isherwood and Stuart[38] note that the Hellenism of the Roman Empire was not so much characterised by a hatred of the body as by the belief that it was radically different from the soul, prone to decay and, therefore, the antithesis of divinity and perfection. It was this burden from which the soul needed to be freed. Importantly, Isherwood and Stuart point out that whilst early Christianity displayed from its earliest days an ambivalence towards the body, it was never uniform in its attitudes. In a review of the idea of the body in Greek Christianity, Kallistos Ware[39] refers to it as "my enemy and my helper". He also notes that the seven ecumenical councils which met between 325 and 787, and which, after the bible, represented doctrinal authority for Greek Christianity, made no formal declarations on the subject.

---

37 The Hebrew scriptures display little hesitation about acknowledging and celebrating the body. Nor do they illustrate any division of the person into parts, or the location of personhood in a disembodied spirit. As ethicist James Nelson says, "They take for granted the goodness of sexuality and at times display lyrical celebrations of the delights of robust, fleshly love". (James B. Nelson, Body Theology (Westminster, 1992), p.31). Kallistos Ware points out that even when the later parts of the Old Testament begin to make tentative references to the afterlife, they do so by envisaging not an immortal soul, but the physical resurrection of the body. (Kallistos Ware, "My enemy and my helper: the body in Greek Christianity" in Coakley (ed.) Religion and the Body).

38 Lisa Isherwood and Elisabeth Stuart, Introducing Body Theology (Sheffield: Sheffield Acad Press, 1998).

39 Ware, in Coakley (ed.) Religion and the Body, p.91.

The writings of the early fathers unsurprisingly reveal an ambivalence concerning the body and show the influence of the gnostic anti-body movements. By contrast, the bodies of martyrs quickly became important sacred relics. When martyrdom, the ultimate expression of the salvific loss of the body, became no longer necessary, the strict asceticism of the desert evolved as an alternative. In his influential work 'The Body and Society', Peter Brown describes this era as a time of deepening insight, although, despite such heroic attempts to escape the carnal realm, desert life itself revealed the "inextricable interdependence of body and soul"[40]. Brown demonstrates that whilst embodied humanity was understood by early Christians in a wide variety of ways, the predominant issue was the dualism connected to sexual renunciation:

> ...by the time Augustine laid down his pen in 430, the leaders of the Christian church already carried in the back of their minds a deposit of assumptions that marked them off irrevocably from the elites of the age.....The Christian notions of sexuality had tended to prise the human person loose from the physical world. The 'calor genitalis', the fiery spirit unleashed in the sexual act, was no longer treated with an ancient reverence. Sexuality was not seen as a cosmic energy that linked human beings both to the fertile herds and to the blazing stars.[41]

Andrew Louth describes the period of Western Catholic Christianity (which only really becomes distinct from Greek language and thought towards the end of the fourth century) as a period of sea-change. The idea of the body moved from being seen as a reflection of the cosmos (sexual activity not just

---

40 Peter Brown, The Body and Society (London: Faber and Faber, 1989), p.236.

41 Ibid, p.432.

as an interpersonal matter, but mirroring the energies of the cosmos) to being seen as the "interpreter of human inwardness"[42]. Here he is principally characterising the contribution of Augustine: "It is in the body, through ascetic endeavour, that the dualities implicit in the fallen human condition are to be overcome"[43]. With the caveat that Augustine is too readily credited with being the principal influence on medieval Latin Christianity, Louth describes a revival of Augustinian theology in the twelfth century, with a consequential dominance of the doctrine of original sin.

In the thirteenth century, says Prokes[44], Aquinas drew heavily on Aristotle's partial affirmations of body-soul unity, but even here, although the soul has sensory aspects which require a connection to the body, the intellect did not depend on the body for its operation. If embodiment was still characterised as a diminishment of the soul's capacity in the high Middle Ages, then there were, according to Prokes, a myriad of external factors that set the stage for the backlash that was the Reformation:

> It is impossible to summarise briefly the melange of attitudes toward the body in the Christian West during the later Middle Ages and the beginning of the 'modern age'. Several critical events, however, have bearing on our survey: the bubonic plague, the abuse of relics and sacramental matter, and the rejection of many aspects of sacramental life among Christians who attempted to eliminate these abuses in life and worship.[45]

---

42 Andrew Louth, in Coakley (ed.) Religion and the Body, p.129.

43 Ibid, p.119

44 Mary Timothy Prokes, Toward a Theology of the Body (Edinburgh: T&T Clark, 1996).

45 Ibid, p.17.

The picture that emerges across these eras is of philosophical and theological influences that were determined to solve the questions of personhood by dualistic routes, whilst never quite being able to ignore the universal, human experience of embodiment. In describing the conception of the body in late antiquity as basically Platonic, Louth suggests that the human body was thought of as a copy or reflection of the cosmos, which itself is a living creature, and achieves health by finding a balance of the three parts of the soul: reason, psychological energy and desire. Sexual energy was to be understood here as a mirror of the energies of the cosmos, with bodies described by Brown as "little fiery universes, through whose heart, brain and veins there pulsed the same heat and vital spirit as glowed in the stars"[46].

In their review of the idea of the medieval body, Mellor and Shilling[47] argue that in the pre-Reformation era any 'official' version of dualism in the Western church should be understood in the context of a religious culture that was emphatically embodied. The culture they describe is one characterised by collective social relationships, which can be thought of as "sacred eating communities"[48]. The pattern was for religious experience that comprised the sacredness immanent in bodies, community and nature. By way of example, the eucharist here is described as the physical incorporation of God into the body of the individual, who in turn is incorporated into the Body of Christ. Mellor and Shilling refer to the feminist historian Margaret Miles' term "carnal knowing"[49], to describe the way in which knowledge,

---

46 Peter Brown, The Body and Society, p.17.

47 Philip Mellor and Chris Shilling, Reforming the Body: religion, community and modernity (London: Sage, 1997).

48 Ibid, p.16.

49 Margaret Miles, Carnal knowing : female nakedness and religious meaning in the Christian west (Tunbridge Wells : Burns & Oates, 1992).

40

experience and understanding should be understood in the medieval era as embodied:

> Bodily experiences did not have to be considered cognitively, and then conceptualised and evaluated by the mind before they could be made sense of...... Knowledge was gained instead from a thinking body in which sensuous understanding involved all of the body's senses, and from the intricate links which existed between the fleshly, physical body and the mind...... It would have appeared nonsensical in these pre-modern times to have suggested that the body was separate, or wholly subordinate to the mind.[50]

In their introduction to feminist theology, Isherwood and Stuart also describe medieval catholicism as sensuous, carnal knowing, "where sanctity and sinfulness could literally be smelt"[51]. Arguably, it was perhaps other manifestations of the medieval church's involvement with the body that preoccupied the Reformers. Wholly embodied for them was its involvement in violence as an instrument of authority, and its willingness to accommodate superstition in an era of murderous religious intolerance.

In any case, Mellor and Shilling describe the Protestant movement as seeking to "abstract" believers from the material and social environment, and to promote instead a personal faith system based on a "committed and fundamentally cognitive engagement with the Word of God"[52]. The pattern is of a move to associations of faith based on shared commitments to articles of belief, rather than communities of bodily interaction. One important

---

50 Mellor and Shilling, Reforming the Body: religion, community and modernity, p.23.

51 Isherwood and Stuart, Introducing Body Theology, p.11.

52 Mellor and Shilling, Reforming the Body: religion, community and modernity, p.98.

implication is the consequential transformation of the idea of the sacred, which becomes "something more sublime; existing but defying satisfactory representation, and encouraging estrangement rather than incorporation"[53]. Here, God becomes "radically transcendent" and the possibility of encountering the sacred in the physical world is removed. Although the idea of the body as sinful had accrued by this time a long Christian history, Mellor and Shilling argue that Protestantism developed it to a new intensity. The overall result was a far deeper relegation of the body, where relating to God became more of an abstract pursuit.:

> As the Reformation progressed, the sensuality and volatility characteristic of the medieval body, and the carnal knowledge gained from a mind immersed in the body's senses, were both stigmatised. In their place, the Protestants promoted a form of cognitive apprehension which required the guilty, sinful body to be disciplined and stilled.[54]

Mellor and Shilling acknowledge that this picture is something of a caricature, and that, for example, Calvin's theology might be said to be community-minded. Accepting this, they argue that, nonetheless, this version of embodied faith is to be understood as a worldly association and therefore inauthentic as compared to the individual's relationship with the Word of God. Isherwood and Stuart note that Luther imagined heaven to be "a place of dancing" and that Zwingli was "convinced of the value of the human body in the sight of God, particularly emphasising the church's

---

53 Ibid, p106.

54 Ibid, p.124.

nature as the body of Christ"[55]. David Tripp[56] argues that both Luther and Zwingli share a "vigorous appreciation" of the physical and communal body but that subsequent Protestant theology has hardly been conscious of it.

The flesh made word

While Mellor and Shilling make mention of the new ways in which the Reformers invested faith and the sacred with a linguistic and textual character (turning religion into "language, thought and text"[57]), they perhaps fail to acknowledge adequately the degree to which the Reformation was dependent on the wider development of written and printed culture. Practically, the Reformation was a movement that was made possible by the powers of the printing press. The reformers benefited from being part of the first religious or secular movement able to exploit the potential of the printed word as a mass medium, and to use it over and against an established institution. There had been many previous schisms within the Western church, but this was the first to be in a position to promulgate its message so widely. Historians have described the ways in which the development of printing and the spread of literacy fuelled the Reformation (for an extended discussion see Eisenstein, 1979[58]). Luther himself described printing as "God's highest and extremest act of grace, whereby the business of the gospel is driven forward"[59]. Of particular interest here are the changes

---

55 Isherwood and Stuart, Introducing Body Theology, p.69.

56 David Tripp, in Coakley (ed.) Religion and the Body, p.142, 147.

57 Mellor and Shilling, Reforming the Body: religion, community and modernity, p.101.

58 Elisabeth Eisenstein, The Printing Press an an Agent of Change (Cambridge: Cambridge University Press, 1979).

59 Ibid, p.431.

associated with printed culture brought about in psychological structures as they impinge on religious experience. This has been most thoroughly explored by Walter Ong, whose work examines the contrasts between oral and written cultures, and the move to "visualism" which gained momentum through the Middle Ages, and beyond:

> In the sixteenth century, as we have seen, the residually oral institutions of dialectic and rhetoric competed strenuously with the new visualism induced by print, for control of man's sensibility, forcing a reorganisation of the sensorium which was changing man's "feel" for his life world. Given the initial importance of the word in Christian teaching - God's word, written in the scriptures and spoken in preaching, and the word of God incarnate in Jesus Christ - it is hardly surprising that many of the critical religious differences among Christians at this time in one way or another, directly or indirectly, register the changing structures surrounding the word.... This can be seen in a multiplicity of developments, among which we can select four groupings: 1) attitudes toward scripture and tradition 2) attitudes towards the sacraments 3) attitudes toward the preaching of the word and 4) attitudes toward authority.[60]

Ong describes a change in the whole nature of religious knowledge whereby it becomes locked on the page, creating the possibility of faith as something that can be "deposited". Ong calls this a "psychological breakthrough of the first order. It embedded the word itself deeply in the manufacturing process and made it into a kind of commodity."[61] For Ong, oral cultures had hitherto assimilated faith "thematically and formulaicly, tribally rather than

60 Ong, The Presence of the Word, p.265.
61 Walter Ong, Orality and Literacy (London: Methuen, 1982), p.118.

individually"[62]. By contrast, the widespread possibility of personal reading "forced the individual into himself and out of the tribe[63]". This development contributed, says Ong, to individualism associated with interior consciousness as something private and religiously neutral, where the mind was "encouraged to sense that its possessions were held in some sort of inert mental space"[64].

For the worshipping community, the understanding of what happens at the eucharist was transformed into an emphasis on how words affect the hearer, rather than the external, embodied event. The availability of printed texts shifted the believer's focus to the words themselves, written or preached, and away from other non-verbal symbolism. Post-typographical Christianity was, says Ong, a religious culture which de-emphasised interpersonal relationships and emphasised visuality with its preference for objectivity and uniformity in the quest for truth and where spontaneity, growth and adaptation of the liturgy could be controlled. The written word, argues Ong in his comparison of orality and literacy, separates *the knower* from *the known* and thus sets up conditions for "objectivity" in the sense of personal disengagement or distancing.[65]

As Eisenstein describes, a negative impact of democratising the availability of sacred texts was to create ever new possibilities for the splintering of the corporeal community of faith:

---

62 Ong, The Presence of the Word, p.269.

63 Ibid, p.270.

64 Ong, Orality and Literacy, p.132.

65 Ibid, p.46.

Stubbornly dogmatic and even obsessive religious attitudes were fostered among the new sects who elevated the infallible scripture to a more lofty position than Catholics ever elevated their popes. An introverted spiritual life developed among solitary readers who received silent guidance from repeatedly re-reading the same book on their own.... open books leading to closed minds?....The rich and variegated communal religious experiences of the middle ages provided a different basis for the 'common culture' of Western man than did the new reliance on bible reading. The impact of printing on the Western scriptural faith thus pointed in two quite opposite directions - toward 'Erasmian' trends and ultimately higher criticism and modernism, and toward more rigid orthodoxy culminating in literal fundamentalism and Bible Belts.[66]

In identifying vision-centred interpretation of religious truth as a contributor to the post-Reformation retreat from the body, we see some consistency with the broad Western philosophical tradition which was our original point of reference. More recent thought finds 'ocularcentrism' at the heart of all human sciences. Western culture, says Kavanagh, may be characterised as an "ocularcentric paradigm, based as it is on a vision-generated, vision-centred interpretation of knowledge, truth and reality."[67] Kavanagh describes the Platonic differentiation between the eye and the "eye of the mind" as foundational for modern thought. He notes that the much later focus-figure of mind-body dualism, Descartes, articulated his alternative to the illusory visible world (the power of reason) with another visual metaphor – the mind's eye, where the properties of the visible world are transferred into

---

66 Eisenstein, The Printing Press an an Agent of Change, p.366.

67 Donncha Kavanagh, Ocularcentrism and its Others in Organisation Studies 25(3) (London: Sage Publications, 2004), p.446.

thought. Descartes may, of course, be said ultimately to have ushered in the era of mind-body dualism ("It is to the body alone that we should attribute everything that can be observed in us to oppose our reason"[68]). However, Kavanagh also argues for enhancements provided by the discovery of perspectivism in the sixteenth century, and by Newton's optical research in the seventeenth century - the single eye at the centre of the visible world:

> This infatuation with the visual reached a new zenith during the Enlightenment (a term that is itself based on an ocular metaphor) when the rationalist understanding that the mind's eye (Reason) could potentially 'see' the Truth came to dominate intellectual thought...... What is interesting for our purposes is that many of the Enlightenment's central precepts, such as objectivism, reflection, critical rationality, and subjectivism, are fundamentally based on the primacy accorded to the visual. In particular, the dominant ocularcentric paradigm promulgated during the Enlightenment worked to elevate static Being over dynamic Becoming and fixed essences over ephemeral appearances.[69]

Ocularcentrism has been severely criticised by twentieth century philosophers, and by French thinkers in particular. According to Jay[70], Sartre had "ocularphobia" and Merleau-Ponty offered a "ceaseless critique of the Cartesian perspectivalist scopic regime [with] its privileging of an ahistorical, disinterested subject entirely outside of the world"[71]. In his recent influential

---

68 Descartes, Selected Philosophical Writings, (Cambridge: Cambridge University Press, 1988), p.236.

69 Donncha Kavanagh, Ocularcentrism and its Others, p.448.

70 Martin Jay, The Denegration of Vision in 20th Century French Thought (1994) Cited by Pallusmaa, see below.

71 Martin Jay, "Scopic Regimes of Modernity" in Hal Foster (ed), Vision and Visuality (Seattle: Bay Press, 1988), p.10. Cited by Pallasmaa, see below.

critique of ocularcentric architecture, Juhani Pallasmaa concludes that Heidegger, Foucault and Darrida have all argued that modernity has furthered the negative tendencies of the ocular bias, reinforced by technology and the proliferation of images:

> The hegemony of sight first brought forth glorious visions, in Heidegger's view, but it has turned increasingly nihilistic in modern times .... The hegemonic eye seeks domination over all fields of cultural production, and it seems to weaken our capacity for empathy, compassion and participation with the world. The narcissistic eye views architecture as a means of self-expression and as an intellectual-artistic game detached from essential mental and societal connections, whereas the nihilistic eye deliberately advances sensory and mental detachment and alienation. Instead of reinforcing one's body-centred and integrated experience of the world, nihilistic architecture disengages and isolates the body.... The world becomes a hedonistic but meaningless visual journey.[72]

More attention will be paid to the Pallasmaa's critique of ocularcentrism in architecture, and its relevance for the visual experience of the worshipping community in the next chapter.

The word made flesh

The Enlightenment produced a thought world overwhelmingly dominated by the ideal of human reason as the only authentic source of understanding

---

72 Juhani Pallasmaa, The Eyes of the Skin, (Chichester: Wiley, 2005), p.22.

the external world. This was a world comprising objective matter that could be investigated, categorised and controlled by the powers of human understanding and ingenuity. It is, therefore, unsurprising that, as Isherwood and Stuart say, "Many theologians of all denominations in the modern period capitulated to this dualism, with the body ceasing to have any ultimate value or purpose in redemption"[73]. As has been described in the first chapter, much of the church architecture and liturgical practice that we are used to now in the West reflects a fundamentally dualistic theology, despite the best efforts of the twentieth-century Liturgical Movement. And yet, even the fragmentary review here of Christian tradition's journey with the idea of the body suggests that committed dualism has never been unreservedly adhered to. Indeed, there are important historical examples of theologies and spiritualities that articulate more integrated models. These have undergone a renaissance in recent years to the point where body-soul dualism has become something of a minority view.

The *Rule of St Benedict* is a sixth-century handbook written as guidance for Benedict's own community of monks at Monte Cassino. In the introduction to her commentary on the rule Esther De Waal comments:

> I have been grateful for the way in which St Benedict recognises the whole of my person as God-given. This is utterly different from that disastrous dualism which influenced my own earlier years, by which the material and the spiritual were set apart and the material, including the bodily, was denigrated and treated as inferior. My upbringing told me that God was only concerned with my soul, and the spiritual side of life was of infinitely more significance than the

---

73 Isherwood and Stuart, Introducing Body Theology, p.72.

bodily. But the rule not only allows but actually encourages me to see my body as worthy of care and nurture, and to be honoured as one element of the whole balance of body, mind and spirit, playing its part in the daily rhythm of work, study and prayer which St Benedict establishes as the way to the fullness of our humanity...... In this holistic approach to life Benedict is speaking a language which has resonances with much of the thought of other traditions, about which there is now such widespread interest. In the Celtic tradition, for example, but also in the Aboriginal or the Native American, we find a unified view of the universe in which religion permeates and informs the whole of life. The sense of the sacredness of material creation, the role of harmony and balance and interrelatedness, for example, are all themes that are apparent the longer that one stays with the rule. A spirituality which is essentially corporate, and addressed the totality of life, is very much in tune with the contemporary attempt to rediscover a unity of vision lost with the dualistic and mechanistic approach which has shaped thinking since the Enlightenment.[74]

De Waal describes a host of examples of this spirituality in the everyday details of, for example, prayer times (where reference is made to accommodating the rhythms of the seasons and of bodily functions), store-keeping, communal and seasonal eating, hospitality, clothing, hygiene, and manual work as an expression of worship and stewardship of what God the creator has provided. Elsewhere, De Waal[75] finds a similar, unified vision in

74 Esther De Waal, A Life Giving Way: a commentary on the Rule of St Benedict (London: Chapman, 1995), p.xiv.

75 Esther De Waal, The Celtic Vision: selectioned and edited from the Carmina Gadelica (London: DLT, 1988).

the Celtic spirituality of the *Carmina Gadelica:* prayers, hymns and poetry collected orally in the outer Hebrides between 1860 and 1900 by Alexander Carmichael. This material represents oral tradition which is traceable to as early as the seventeenth century but which is presumed to be much earlier, having emerged from the spirituality of the early Celts, whose theologians followed their druid ancestors in seeing all things as impregnated with spirit (something they transformed by using the framework of the Trinity). Here again, De Waal explores devotional material that celebrates the divine presence in all things bodily and material, and where all physical activities "become the occasion for praying and for involving the heavenly powers.... there is no divide here between this world and the next. Heaven and earth are interconnected and interacting"[76]. As an example of this unity, De Waal quotes the following prayer:

> I believe, O Lord and God of the peoples,
>
> That thou art He who created my soul and set its warp,
>
> Who created my body from dust and ashes,
>
> Who gave to my body breath, and to my soul its possession.
>
> Father, bless to me my body,
>
> Father, bless to me my soul,
>
> Father, bless to me my life,
>
> Father, bless to me my belief.[77]

Latter-day Christian Celt, George MacLeod, may be credited with one strand of the current resurgence in Celtic spirituality. As founder of the Iona Community, MacLeod's unifying mission was the tackling of the destructive breakdown, as he saw it, between peoples, between churches, between

---

76 Ibid, p.8.

77 Ibid, p.20. Quoted from the Carmina Gadelica.

humanity and the earth, and between spirit and matter. For MacLeod, one of whose favourite sayings was "matter matters", the essential quality of the material is the spiritual, and reverence for the created order defines spirituality[78]. J.Philip Newell identifies the two main features of Celtic spirituality as "the belief that what is deepest in every human being is the image of God, and the belief that creation is essentially a disclosure or self-giving of God."[79] Elsewhere, describing MacLeod's christology he says:

> Shining through the material world is the spiritual world that upholds it and enlivens it. Christ reveals to us what is at the heart of matter. Hidden in the mystery of our own bodies and the body of all creation is the unseeable One, glory of the everlasting world.[80]

Body-affirming theology of this kind may be categorised as 'incarnational'. If, as the prologue to John's Gospel says, "all things came into being through the Word", and "the Word became flesh and dwelt among us", then the human body is, says Newell, "a sacred text within the larger text of creation[81]". The prologue may be said to declare the dignity of Christ's embodiment, which is the ultimate realisation of human vocation. Incarnational theology emphasises that the most decisive experience of God is not in the credal or propositional realm, but in the Word made flesh and in the Word still becoming flesh. Timothy Gorringe goes so far as to argue that body-soul dualism denies God a body. We are, he says, endowed with senses by God so that God can explore creation: "God chooses embodiment, and not

---

78 For a summary of MacLeod's life and spirituality see: Ronald Ferguson, George MacLeod, founder of the Iona Community (London: Collins, 1990).

79 J. Philip Newell, in Coracle: Journal of the Iona Community (October 2004), p.5.

80 J. Philip Newell, Echo of the Soul (Canterbury: Morehouse/Canterbury Press, 2000), p.106.

81 Ibid, p.xv.

just in Christ. God chooses materiality in the first place, according to Genesis. That is God's option. This is counter-intuitive to the Greek tradition."[82]

In his account of post-war liturgical renewal, John Robinson sees the issue of sanctity in worship as a function of incarnational thinking:

> Such was the difference which the Incarnation had made, when God himself had called all things holy; and it is this difference of which the sacraments are the standing embodiment and reminder. But for this reason they remain, or should remain, a standing offence to any mentality that would still like to drive a wedge between the holy and the common...... If at the very heart of our religion, in our celebration of the 'holy mysteries', we enshrine the Jewish conception of a 'holy of holies', then it will not be the religion of the Incarnation, nor will we know its power.[83]

In an earlier book, Robinson argues that the body is the central, defining concept at the heart of Pauline theology:

> It is from the body of sin and death that we are delivered; it is through the body of Christ on the cross that we are saved; it is into the body of the church that we are incorporated; it is by his body in the eucharist that the community is sustained; it is in our body that its new life has to be manifest; it is to a resurrection of this body to the likeness of his glorious body that we are destined.[84]

82 Timothy Gorringe, The Education of Desire (London: SCM, 2001), p.9.

83 JAT Robinson, Liturgy Coming To Life (London: Mowbray, 1960), p.39.

84 JAT Robinson, The Body: a study in Pauline theology (London: SCM, 1952).

For the worshipping community, the recurring challenge is to reflect the spirit of the New Testament writers, who are generally aligned with the unitary approach of their Hebraic heritage, whose scriptures abound in graphic accounts of how the body is involved in divine revelation. The incarnational intervention is central, particularly because the salvation associated with it is visibly offered through the life and death of Christ, physically born, who physically laboured, hungered and suffered, and who knew the physical and emotional consequences of relatedness. Even amidst the other-worldliness of the resurrection narratives, the gospels insist on the physicality of Christ's risen body. Kallistos Ware argues that it is a mistake to think of Paul as a dualist. The contrast Paul makes is not between *soma* and *psyche*, but between *sarx* and *pneuma*. The distinction is that the latter contrast refers to personhood in its totality rather than components of the individual. 'Flesh' is the whole person as fallen, and 'spirit' is the whole person as redeemed:

> Whilst Paul's view of the flesh is sombre, his estimate of the body is highly affirmative. "Present your bodies as a living sacrifice to God", he writes (Rom 12;1). "Your body is a temple of the Holy Spirit..... Glorify God in your body" (1 Cor 6:19-20). That is exactly why sexual promiscuity is so deplorable - not because the body and its sexuality are unclean but because they are potentially holy: "Your bodies are members of Christ" (1 Cor 6:15). This vital Pauline distinction between sarx and soma has unfortunately been overlooked by all too many preachers and moralists in later times, and so they have assumed that his strictures about the flesh apply to the body as such. The pastoral consequences have been depressing.[85]

---

85 Ware, in Coakley (ed.) Religion and the Body, p.94.

Newell agrees that the mistake of equating body and flesh has had "disastrous consequences" in the loss of the intended Pauline invitation "to be liberated, to be reconciled to what is deepest in us instead of being held in bondage to what is false in us."[86] These views principally refer to the issue of human sexuality, and it is around the debate about this aspect of personhood that 'Body Theology' has developed, coming into prominence in the 1960's. Christian ethicist, James Nelson, associates this with the sexual revolution of that decade and suggests that body experience should always be understood as sexual experience. It is, he says, part of being in the world:

> ....as body-selves who are gendered biologically and socially, who have varying sexual orientations, who have the capacity for sensuousness, who have the need for intimacy, who have varied and often conflicting feelings about what it means to be bodied. It is all of this body experience that is foundational to our moral agency; our capacities for action and power, our abilities to tolerate ambiguity, and our capacities for moral feeling. Our bodily experience significantly colours our interpretations of the social relationships, communities and institutions which are the stuff of ethics.[87]

It is, says Nelson, particularly the feminist and gay liberation movements which have reminded us of the important place of bodily experience in Christian theology, and it is male theologians in particular who have been guilty of locating theology in the realm of spirit and mind. Religious feminism has critiqued ways in which the church has therefore typically been a patriarchal community in its language, its worship, its theological imagery, its patterns of leadership and its ethics. Largely patriarchal worship

86 Newell, Echo of the Soul, p.xiii.

87 James B. Nelson, Body Theology (Westminster, 1992), p.45.

patterns have consequently been characterised by a masculine concentration on word, and a suspicion of bodily feelings. Again, such characteristics are all too visibly played out in the architectural and ritual arrangements of the Western tradition. For the worshipping community, the key feminist emphasis on the centrality of relationship could inspire what Beverley Wildung Harrison calls the "spirituality of sensuality" in the working out and expression of its corporate life:

> As a feminist moral theology celebrates the power of our human praxis as an intrinsic aspect of the work of God's love, as it celebrates the reality that our moral-selves are body-selves who touch and see and hear each other into life, recognising sensuality as fundamental to the work and power of love, so above all else, a feminist moral theology insists that relationality is at the heart of all things.[88]

The argument is that such relationality should, likewise, be at the heart of worship practice, with all of the attendant liturgical and ritual implications. The underlying proposal will be that thoroughgoing fleshly encounter is acknowledged as vitally important to the worshipper's experience of God.

Worshipper dissonance, corporeal flux and felt response

In concluding this discussion I would argue that worship practice which fails to address the assumption of religious dualism risks the possibility of dissonance. This is particularly true in a context where the human sciences and the sense of fragmentation and artificiality that characterises aspects of

88 Beverly Wildung Harrison, The Power of Anger in the Work of Love: Christian ethics for women and other strangers, in Union Seminary Quarterly Review 36 Supp.(1981), p.45

contemporary culture have led to a renewed interest in mind-body integration. The highly rationalised environments associated with modernity, say Mellor and Shilling, have ultimately evoked a nostalgia for, and a resurgence of interest in, more sensual ways of understanding the external world:

> Ultimately, perhaps, people find cultures which have become banal unbearable, and seek instead opportunities to reconsecrate the profane. The renewed interest in fate, destiny, the stars, magic, tarot, nature, cults and games of chance appear to reflect this.[89]

Mellor and Shilling are rigorous in blaming Protestantism for deconstructing the "organic fusion" that characterised medieval religion and society. Pointing to the analyses of Durkheim and Weber of the post-Reformation spiritual disorganisation of Europe, they argue that the associated depreciation of ritual and the abstraction of people from natural, supernatural and social environments is a major contributor to the development of individualism.

If, as has already been discussed, this is paralleled in worship practice, the problem of what Mellor and Shilling call "corporeal flux"[90] is of particular interest. By this, they mean the problem for believers in connecting with their body-selves, in a religious environment where strong emotions are interpreted as weakness or sin.[91] For theologies of the body, such disconnectedness from body-mediated knowledge means disconnectedness

---

89 Mellor and Shilling, Reforming the Body: religion, community and modernity, p.26.

90 Ibid, p.98.

91 Ibid, p.121. Mellor and Shilling offer Durkheim's description of "anomie" as an example of the potential for body-soul dissonance in Protestantism: "In making God radically transcendent, thus transforming the sacred into the sublime, they removed the possibility of directly encountering the sacred in the world".

from moral and meaningful human action. Harrison argues that one of feminist theology's principal contributions is to address the distortions of body-mind dualism which assume detachment as a precondition for moral action:

> ...we recognise that all our knowledge , including our moral knowledge, is body-mediated knowledge. All knowledge is rooted in our sensuality. We know and value the world, if we know and value it, through our ability to touch, to hear, and to see. Perception is foundational to conception. Ideas are dependent on our sensuality. Feeling is the basic bodily ingredient which mediated our connectedness to the world. When we cannot feel, literally, we lose our connection to the world. All power, including intellectual power, is rooted in feeling. If feeling is damaged or cut off, our power to image the world and act into it is destroyed and our rationality is impaired...... Failure to live deeply 'in our bodies, ourselves' destroys the possibility of moral relations between us.[92]

The implication is that worship practice will also nurture a debilitating dissonance if experience is less than body-mediated. Knowledge of God, individual and corporate spirituality, and relatedness to the world and the community are dependent on this view, upon a unified worship experience, fed by all dimensions of the perceptive self.

In a later study of the theology and ethics of embodiment, James Nelson coincides with Harrison in identifying feeling as the measure of authenticity of religious or moral being. Thus, "if I can't feel injustice, I cannot really perceive injustice, even if I have learned from others how to name it and

---

92 Harrison, The Power of Anger in the Work of Love, p.48.

what it looks like"[93]. In much the same way, we may say that if the worshipper cannot feel the love of God for the world, the divine outrage at injustice, the relatedness of the worshipping community, or the passion and compassion of the reconciling Christ, then these dynamics are experienced in the worship environment as learned responses only. Nelson appeals to the work of Charles Davis on the idea of embodied religious feeling. Davis begins by defining the feeling response, which is to be distinguished from the emotional response, in that it is more than a bodily reaction to a physical or imaginative stimulus. The feeling response is spiritual, rational and affective, as well as bodily: "There is no feeling without bodily motion, any more than there is intellectual knowledge without the participation of sense and imagination"[94]. To be religious therefore, says Davis, is to have religious feelings, which is not a necessary condition for the adherence to or study of religious ideas:

> ....the fundamental religious experience is the total, connatural response of ourselves as embodied persons to religious reality and value. It would follow that we should encourage and train the bodily component of our affectivity, direct and refine it, so that it becomes the medium of religious meaning. Instead, we are met, apparently with a negation of bodiliness and sensuousness. We are asked to exclude our affectivity. There is little or no acknowledgement of the processes of material mediation implied by our complex make up as embodied persons. In brief, there is seemingly a reaching after a pure immateriality of religious response[95].

---

93 James B. Nelson, Embodiment (London: SPCK, 1979), p.31.

94 Charles Davis, Body as Spirit: the nature of religious feeling (London: Hodder, 1976), p.6.

95 Ibid, p.36.

Davis' distinctions are attractive for those in Western worship traditions who instinctively recoil from forms that nurture emotion or sensuality. In contrast to the emotional, the felt response is embodied, intelligent and affective, involving a cognitive apprehension of experience, and "an insightful relationship with what is felt". Davis makes a further useful distinction between the desirable qualities of 'sensuousness' (an openness to the spontaneous rhythms and responses of the body, over and above the detached observation and assessment of intellectual response) and 'sensuality' (the submission of the body so as to use it as an instrument of pleasure, where the body, driven by the mind, is alienated from its own spontaneous rhythms). Of relevance for the worship paradigm is Davis' suggestion that sensuousness is associated with sacramental or mystical experience whereas sensuality inhibits symbolic potential in reducing reality to physicality. A sensuous or felt worship form, then, is one that allows for the mutual participation of human consciousness and physical phenomena:

> Interpreted by human consciousness, they also serve as hierophanies or manifestations of the holy, transcendent reality in which they participate........ In the context of that relationship with the physical world, bodily sensuous experience becomes a vehicle for the mystical. The spontaneity of the body becomes the outward form and perceptible presence of the spontaneity of the spirit.[96]

To rediscover the body in this way is, for Davis, no less than to rediscover our openness to reality, and my thesis is that the awakening of sensory awareness in the forms and practices of the worshipping community is fundamental to experience that is both holistic and creative. The experience

---

96 Ibid, p.42.

of ritual events and places as sacred is to be understood as a consequence of the interaction brought about by the spontaneous, felt responses of unavoidably embodied worshippers. Remaining parts of this study will attempt to explore some of the sensorial dynamics of environments for worship, and there to identify spatial forms and liturgical practice that promote or inhibit incarnational, embodied experience.

Chapter Three

Seeing is believing

Introduction

I have argued that an affective, sensuous worshipper-response is associated with theology, environmental forms and worship practices which allow for and promote the centrality of whole-body experience. My proposal is that the worshipping community should consider more carefully the nature of embodied experience in at least some of the ways in which the body is typically involved in worship rituals. Drawing on physical and psycho-physical perspectives, I will discuss in the following two chapters something of the experiential nature of visual and auditory perception, and propose some implications for an embodied approach to the worship environment. In the first of these I will argue for a re-emphasis of concepts that I will characterise as *material light* and *unfocused vision*, proposing these as norms for the worshipping community.

Let There Be Light

> All material in nature, the mountains and the streams and the air and we, are made of light which has been spent, and this crumpled mass called material casts a shadow, and the shadow belongs to light. *Louis Khan*[97]

---

97 Louis Kahn, quoted in John Lobell, <u>Between Silence and Light: spirit in the architecture of Louis I. Kahn,</u> (Boston: Shaubhala, 1985), p.5.

Architecture is the correct and magnificent play of masses brought together in light. *Le Corbusier*[98]

Light, God's eldest daughter, is a principle beauty in a building. *Thomas Fuller*[99]

Consideration has already been given to the hegemony of the visual in Western thought and the extent to which this has dominated philosophy and Christian doctrine. Ironically, this ocular bias has been described as a major influence upon the loss of the body and the consequent growth of individualism, alienation and detachment. Vision, as we have seen, has been emphatically associated with understanding and light has come to be the predominant metaphor for truth. Perception itself is commonly understood to refer to cognitive apprehension, or what we might call 'insight' (inner vision). We have seen that these associations have been profoundly integrated into the Christian tradition and that they have contributed to the complex history of dualism that has been described here.

However, using such ocular language, we may also say that it is clear that human experience is inextricably woven with the physical process of visual perception. It is normative (with the obvious exception of those who are visually impaired or blind) for us to move through the world on the basis of a complex flow of information, a significant part of which is visual. Visual perception itself (which, as we will see, is a much more complex process than simply registering retinal data) is but one of the ways that the body is in receipt of the life-giving properties of light. Solar energy is at the heart of the

---

98 Charles Jeanneret (Le Corbusier), Towards a New Architecture (New York: Praeger, 1946).

99 Thomas Fuller, Holy and Profane States, (Book III, "Of Building", 1642)

created universe; there can, after all, be no life without its power. It follows that an integrated, whole-body worship approach should be one that celebrates and explores the nature of both physical light and visual perception, so as to recover their role in the provision of worship environments that authentically enrich the sense of being and of self.

According to John Lobell, the influential American architect Louis Kahn (1901-1974) turned for inspiration "to the eternal, to that which transcends the circumstances of any given moment, where he found order and from which he brought spirit back into our world"[100]. Kahn used the word 'light' to mean 'pure being', as yet without material quality. When making an architectural drawing, he observed that the material world begins where light stops – usually where a drawn line represents a wall. The material world is, he said, "light that has spent itself".

This distinction between material and immaterial light has been a familiar theme both in the history of Western philosophical thought, as has already been mentioned above, and in religious systems across time and cultures. Precisely because of its life-giving powers, light has always been associated with the divine. In the ancient world, fear of darkness and reverence for the sun as master of the seasons inspired well-known monuments and religious sites, such as Stonehenge and the Egyptian pyramids. The divinisation of light is well represented in the scriptural traditions of world religions: Buddhist writings contain an overwhelming number of references to the Buddha as Divine Light; and the Qur'an is specific about Allah as the source of light. In Jewish mysticism, particularly in the Kabbalah and in Philo of

---

100 Lobell, Between Silence and Light, p.4.

Alexandria (heavily influenced by Hellenistic thought), the utterly brilliant Divine Light is visible only to the 'mind's eye'.

The effect of immaterial light – the means of creation, incarnation, and salvation

The Hebrew scriptures begin with what Brueggemann calls a "poetic narrative"[101], a theological affirmation of creation written for, and serving as, an exilic refutation of Babylonian theological claims:

> Darkness was upon the face of the deep. And God said; "let there be light" and there was light. And God saw that the light was good; and God separated the light from the darkness. God called the light day, and the darkness he called night.
>
> *Genesis 1:2-3*

Of particular significance for the Judaeo-Christian tradition is the fact that this giving of light is the first act of creation. In his commentary Von Rad calls light "the first born of creation": "Without light there is no creation; only light reveals the contours of the creature blurred in darkness"[102]. He emphasises the "creatureliness" of light in Genesis, essentially distinct from, but belonging to, God. For Westermann the Genesis material is unique among creation narratives in using the separation of darkness and light as the template for temporal order – the succession of days, which demonstrates the precedence of time over space. The designation of light as 'good' (a designation not shared by the darkness) reveals, he says, God's

---

101 Walter Brueggemann, Genesis: in The Bible Commentary for Teaching and Preaching (Atlanta: John Knox Press, 1982)

102 Gerhard Von Rad, Genesis (London: SCM, 1961), p.51.

"prejudice" toward light[103]. For both commentators, the approval of light is associated not with aesthetics but with purpose and salvation. It is, says Westermann, an immediate, first hint of a trend that will shape the "whole story of the created world".

Although not equated with God in the creation accounts, light does subsequently accompany theophanies in the patriarchal narratives (for example, in Genesis 15:12). In the prophetic tradition there are examples of 'knowledge of God' and of 'wisdom' as the light of life, whilst the poetic literature abounds with imagery that expresses how God provides light to those who walk his ways[104]. Jesus uses this imagery in the synoptic Gospels: "You are the light of the world... let your light shine before others, so that they may see your good works and give glory to your Father in heaven" (Matthew 5:14ff). In Luke's Gospel, Jesus compares "the sons of this age" with "the sons of light" (16:8). In both of the accounts of the transfiguration (Matthew 17:2-5 and Mark 9:2ff) the authentication of Jesus' divine essence and mission is demonstrated by the appearance of his physical body and clothes as pure or unfiltered light.

It is not until the Neo-Platonic era of the Johanine literature that light is specifically identified with God and used as a metaphor for Christ and his mission. It is one of the key metaphors of John's Gospel, where it appears twenty one times. Schnackenburg argues that the first chapter prologue to the Gospel links Jesus with the creation narratives:

---

103 Claus Westermann, Genesis 1-11 : a continental commentary (Minneapolis:Fortress Press, 1994), p.8.

104 For example: Ps 27:1 "The Lord is my light and my salvation"; 36:9 "..in your light we see light"; 37:6 "He will make your vindication shine like the light"; 97:11 "Light dawns for the righteous"; 104:2 "You are clothed with honour and majesty, wrapped in light as with a garment"; 119:105 "Your word is a lamp to my feet and a light to my path"; Isaiah 60:1 "Arise, shine; for your light has come, and the glory of the Lord has risen upon you....nations shall come to your light, and kings to the brightness of your dawn".

Jesus is the "light of the world" in so far as he makes it possible to possess the "light of life" (8:12). Hence the "light" also evokes the notion of the eschatological salvation, which is another link with the Jewish world of the Old Testament. The activity of the logos as "light" begins with creation and extends by means of the Incarnation to the eschatological fulfilment. Indeed from the very beginning, it is aimed at bringing men home to God's world of light.[105]

According to Barrett, life and light were both terms which characterised Hellenistic religious and philosophical thought, since many of the popular religions were based on mythologies that addressed the conflict between light and darkness. 'God as light' is the basic assumption of the oriental inspired gnostic religions. This influence, emanating principally from Persia, says Barrett, moved through the Roman Empire with diverse effects, including belief in divinised men (often portrayed as the source of rays of light): "The light here brought into the process of revelation is the primal light, the beginning of Hermetic cosmogony."[106] Barrett claims that it is even possible to find other examples of unions between the divine Father and Son that are "very close" to John's thought: "..a collocation of light and life, of the cosmological and revealing functions of the Word, who is the Son of God and the light of men"[107]. Consistent with Schnackenburg's view (as well as Westermann and Von Rad's purposeful creation-light) Barrett states that "light of the world" as used by John describes a soteriological function. Thus light is not a metaphysical definition of the person of Jesus, but a description of his *effect* upon the cosmos: he is the light which judges and saves it. "In

105 R. Schnackenburg, The Gospel According to St John (London: Burns and Oates, 1968), p.244.

106 C.K.Barrett, The Gospel According to St John (London: SPCK, 1978), p.336.

107 Ibid, p.336.

him only the world has its day.....in his absence is darkness."[108] The light described by Jesus can be *in* others, so that they may become children of the light (John 12:36). The first letter of John restates that the source of saving light is God (1 John 1:5) and uses the image of light as a symbol of Christian living ("walk in the light as he is light"). Further on, at 2:8, the incarnation is characterised as the coming of "true light".

James 1:17 appeals to solar properties, and perhaps the inconsistency of available artificial light, in describing God as "the Father of lights, with whom is no variation or shadow cast by turning". In the Pauline letters too, the writer (whose dramatic conversion experience centred on the blinding effects of exposure to brilliant light associated with the presence of the risen Christ) describes those spiritually reborn into the new faith as "sons of light and sons of the day" (1 Thessalonians 5:5). Indeed, they have in some sense become light itself (Ephesians 5:8).

Having begun by describing light as the first act of creation, the biblical account concludes with the Johanine vision of the heavenly city where the soteriological process is complete. The redeemed realm is characterised as light whose source is Christ. Here, where the most sacred of environments is envisioned, the only form required is light itself:

> I saw no temple in the city, for its temple is the Lord God the
> Almighty and the Lamb. And the city has no need of sun or moon to
> shine on it, for the glory of God is its light, and the lamp is the Lamb.
> The nations will walk by its light, and kings of the earth shall bring
> their glory into it. Its gates will never be shut by day, and there will

---

108 Ibid, p.357.

be no night there.

Revelation 21:22-25

Mention should be made here of the Eastern Church's mystical theology of 'uncreated light'. Here, biblical imagery is understood to provide an expression of real aspects of the godhead. Divine light is neither abstract or allegorical, but is received in mystical experience of the energies or grace in which God makes himself known. This light is immaterial and so is not encountered in the realm of the senses. A full account of this theology is given by Lossky[109].

The effect of material light

This view of light as immaterial is problematic insofar as it contributes to the kind of dualism that has already been described. Light as a metaphor for the divine, is, after all, drawn from the inspiration provided by the experience of physical light. Jesus' identification of himself as the "light of the world" in John 8:12 is delivered against the backdrop of the Feast of Tabernacles (John 7:2). The feast involved the illumination of the Temple from the Court of Women. This area was surrounded by deep galleries of spectators with a view of four great candelabra, which, when lit, were said to light up every courtyard in the city (for a fuller description see Barclay[110]). It is not hard to imagine something of how the effects of this artificial light could have provided inspiration for Jesus' words. Indeed, if the 'illumination' of divine

109 Vladimir Lossky, The Mystical Theology of the Eastern Church (Cambridge: James Clarke, 1957), esp pp.217-235.

110 William Barclay, The Gospel of John, Vol.2 (Edinburgh: St Andrew Press, 1973), p.10ff.

light has significantly appealed to the ocular and dualistic tendency in Christian tradition, then, arguably, the biblical emphasis on the 'effects' of light provide inspiration for prioritising the effects of physical light on integrated mind-body experience and, consequentially, on our use of environments for worship. As a dominant symbol in the biblical accounts of the divine soteriological activity (creation, incarnation and eschaton), the apprehension and use of physical light in the worship environment should never be reduced to the provision of what is practically necessary.

For the physicist, visible light is merely a small part of the electromagnetic spectrum of energy, found between ultra-violet and infra-red radiation. It is this region which is absorbed by the photo-receptors of the human visual system. Importantly, the human eye does not see light, but rather the effects of light, and it is with those effects that the designers and users of designated spaces for worship should be concerned.

The ways in which illumination is provided, and finished surfaces specified, will create the *effects of light* that influence and shape experience. The surfaces that define a given space (the walls, floor, ceiling, glazing, installations, furniture and textures) are themselves transformed by the light they receive. The available light changes as it strikes those surfaces and in this way, environmental space and light are inextricably linked. It is insufficient then to arrange environments for human occupancy (including spaces for worship) and then add lighting as a subsequent process, with the sole purpose of making the environment functional. According to the renowned architectural theorist Walter Gropius, his task was:

...to teach what influences the psyche of man in terms of light, scale, form and colour. Vague phrases like "the atmosphere of a building" or "the cosiness of a room" should be defined precisely in specific terms. The designer must learn to see; he must know the effect of optical illusions, the psychological influence of shapes, colours and textures, the effects of contrast, direction, tension and repose; and he must learn to grasp the significance of the human scale.[111]

Seeing the light - the effects of material light on whole-body experience

When we walk into a designated worship space and instinctively look around, the apprehension of visual information is a deceptively simple, and largely unconscious, participation in a profoundly complex process. Visual perception can fairly be called the primary process by which we acquire our information about the world (accounting for an estimated 80%) and the physiology of the visual system is a relatively well-defined area of knowledge. The effects of light, which are both biological and psychological, require the interaction of 'sensation' and 'perception', whereby the remarkable physiology of the eye serves to provide data for neural interpretation. Some psychologists have called this "physiognomic" perception; that is, the active participation of the brain in the act of seeing, or making sense of what is seen.

This relatively recent contribution of the psychology of perception has hastened a radical departure from the empiricist approach of philosophers

---

111 Walter Gropius, The Scope of Total Architecture (New York: Collier Books, 1970/1943), p.33.

like Hume or Locke, who thought that perceived knowledge was immediately and reliably derived from the physical world. We now know that perceiving the world involves the constant interpretation and filtering of illusions. Perception of size, for example, involves the problem of the discrepancy between what the information from the retina would suggest and the way something may actually appear to the observer (commonly experienced as optical illusions). The ability to affect 'constancy' (for example, the perception that progressively converging railway lines are in fact parallel) is an example of the interpretative function of the visual system that sets it apart from the limitations of the photographic image. This holds true not only for size but for colour, brightness, shape and other qualities. Indeed, the leading sensory psychologist, Richard Gregory, argues that perception may be defined as a series of hypotheses which are tested by knowledge and assumption[112].

Perhaps the most significant factor in visual experience is in fact experienced in the dynamic definition of our walk into the worship environment. Although space is typically measured in three dimensions, human interaction with the environment includes a fourth dimension of time, or of movement through space – the kinaesthetic experience. Not only do human beings explore their environment by moving through it, but even the most static of spaces (say, a historic church building) effects highly significant perceptual changes for a mobile observer due to changing lighting conditions (most obviously the constant revolution of daylight variations and darkness); the powerful light/dark 'adaptation' abilities of the retina; and the resultant modified perception of reflected light as it alters the appearance of distance, colour and texture.

112 Richard Gregory, The Intelligent Eye (London: Weidenfeld and Nicolson, 1970) and Eye and Brain: the psychology of seeing (Oxford: Oxford University Press, 1997).

If the worshipping community's use of its designated environment is to show an awareness of a moving sun, moving people and the effects of material light, as perceived by the human visual system, then I would advocate that further attention be paid to the perception and effect of colour, as well as to the use of natural and artificial lighting.

A word about human visual sensitivity

A small section of the electromagnetic energy of the sun is visible light. This is quantified as light waves of measurable frequencies (nanometers - each unit equal to a billionth of a meter). The colours of different wavelengths can be easily separated out (as in school laboratory experiments with prisms) into violet (380-436nm); blue (430-495nm); green (496-566nm); yellow (566-589nm); and red (627-780nm)[113].

The human eye is a light-sensing system with an adjustable pupil, a lens and a photo-receptive medium, the retina. The retina contains two types of photo-receptors in order to equip us for the two modes of light and darkness. Cones (about 500 million, which are sensitive to bright or 'photopic' light in colour) are responsible for day vision. Rods (about 100 million, which see dim or 'scotopic' light in black and white) are associated with night vision. 'Adaptation' of the retina to different levels of light involves switching between the rods and cones. In dark conditions, the chemical rhodopsin is activated in the rods which take between twenty and sixty minutes to fully assume the reception of available light. At most of the visible wavelengths the human eye is more sensitive than photographic film and can discern

113 Ibid, pp.6-10 for more detail.

differences in the green sector as small as one nanometer. Although an object in direct sunlight may be as much as one million times brighter than the same object illuminated by moonlight, the eye can register both effectively. With age, there is a gradual reduction of the pupil diameter at a given level of adaptation to light. This results in a potential threefold reduction in the amount of light reaching the retina between the ages of twenty and sixty[114]. Light reaching the retina is converted into electrical signals that are transmitted via the optic nerve.

Peak sensitivity and focussed vision occur at the fovea, a relatively small area in the middle of the retina. Points of attention are constantly directed to the fovea by means of rapid eye movements or 'saccades' (from the French "flick of a sail") at a rate of up to four or five per second. Outside the foveal focus, the potential peripheral field of view is sensitive to the presence of objects over an entire hemisphere, especially if they move. For a full account of the physiology of the human visual system see Dreher and Robinson, 1991[115].

The nature and effects of colour perception

As with the perception of light generally, colour perception is not simply a matter of receiving physical stimulation, but a process charged with emotional association, learned response, aesthetic judgement and physiological effects. An embodied worship experience will be one that

---

114 P.R.Boyce, Illuminance, Visual Performance and Preference (in Lighting Research and Technology, 5, 1973), pp.125-140.

115 B.Dreher and S.Robinson (eds.), Vision and Visual Dysfunction/Vol 3 (Houndmills: Macmillan Press, 1991).

acknowledges the effects of colour in the designated environment. In the words of colour theorist Frank Mahnke:

> The first consideration in the creation of interior and exterior architectural spaces must be the evidence that has been accumulated concerning human response to the environment. ... Colour and light are major factors in our architectural environment. They have great impact on our psychological reactions and physiological well being. Research has proven that light and colour affect the human organism on both a visual and non-visual basis. It is no longer valid to assume that the only significant role of light and colour is to provide adequate illumination and a pleasant visual environment.[116]

In the creation and arrangement of environments for worship, therefore, whole-body experience is diminished if the colours of reflected light are assumed to be mere by-products of construction materials. Indeed, the business of 'decorating' the worship space should become a project that amounts to much more than a fabric committee's choices of wall colour based on practical matters of tradition, planning regulation, heritage restriction, unsubstantiated preference, or even the budgetary advantages of a bargain batch of paint.

Human experience of colour should not be thought of in terms of the properties of particular objects, or of particular surfaces in a designated space (say, the red pine communion table against the magnolia sanctuary wall). Rather, it is properly defined as the sensation caused by the qualities of particular and variable light, as recognised by the eye and interpreted by the

---

116 Frank Mahnke, Colour, Environment and Human Response (New York: Van Nostrand Reinhold, 1996), p.3.

76

brain. An embodied approach to worship space will pay careful attention to the psychological, physiological, technical and aesthetic aspects of the colour of reflected light.

Detailed research has been carried out into the effects of colour and associated light sources, especially in horticulture. It is well established that plants, insects and animals display definite colour preferences. For example, commercial cultivation practices can force plants by introducing variations in colour or exposure to light (Ott, 1967[117]). According to Birren, human response is no less significant:

> It may ...be generalised that colour affects muscular tension, cortical activation (brain waves), heart rate, respiration, and other functions of the autonomic nervous system – and certainly that it arouses definite emotional and aesthetic reactions, like and dislikes, pleasant and unpleasant associations.[118]

There are undoubtedly problems associated with research into human colour response because of the subjective nature of the experience; for instance, perception of colour varies between individuals; according to Michel[119] approximately 8% of males and 0.5% of females are affected by some level of colour blindness. Despite these difficulties, however, Mahnke[120] presents a comprehensive review of colour-response studies and proposes a categorising of psychological factors. These fall into two main groups:

---

117 J.N.Ott, Effects of wavelengths of light on physiological functions of plants and animals, (Illuminating Engineer Society, 1967), Colour and Light: their effects on plants, animals and people, (International Journal of Biosocial Research, 7, 1985). Cited by Mahnke.

118 Faber Birren, Light, Colour and Environment (New York: Van Nostrand Reinhold, 1982), p.20.

119 Lou Michel, Light: The Shape of Space (New York: Van Nostrand Reinhold, 1996), p.88.

120 Mahnke, Colour, Environment and Human Response, p.11ff.

1. The biological and unconscious responses are those that are "beyond our control since they are in the physiological realm that remains outside the scope of how we, as individuals, think or feel about a certain hue, or a group of colours."[121] Here Mahnke refers to evolved characteristics whereby the visual system carries light and colour stimulation to the hypothalamic midbrain region, and on to the pineal and pituitary glands. These control the endocrine system and the production and release of hormones. Coloured light also acts through the skin – the use of blue light, for example, to cure infant jaundice has been standard medical practice for decades. Included in this group are those responses which Jung referred to as coming from from the "collective unconscious", or from archetypes within the psyche of the species – primordial and genetic responses.

2. Conscious association responses include cross-cultural consistency (i.e. blue with sky or water, green with nature, red with revolution); local specifics (i.e. national flag colours); and trends in response to consumer boredom. Mahnke counsels caution in use of these colours in architectural space as they typically evoke contextually inappropriate schemes.

121 Ibid, p.13.

The individual's personal relationship to colour, says Mahnke, is a product of the interrelationships among these factors. However, he does assert that there is evidence of a universal "emotional loading":

> Valuable information about emotional content of colours comes from a series of separate psychological experiments conducted by Frieling, Pfister, Luscher, Stefanescu-Goanga[122], and others. Comparisons were made between colour symbolisms found in different culture groups ranging from European Christians to old Egyptian, ancient Chinese, and early Greek. All evidenced ritual symbolism based on the experience of colour in nature. These transferred to and evolved into major emotional associations stimulated by certain colours. These in turn were transferred to sociological-cultural and religious experiences. Deeply ingrained conscious-unconscious connotations of colour are therefore not just a matter of individual interpretation, but part of our collective heritage. All connotations are derived from certain primary associations.[123]

In their influential study in the 1960s, Berlin and Kay[124] demonstrated that basic colour terms are universal. In short, their meanings in different languages both coincide and appear in languages in a certain order. Mahnke summarises universal connotations, including those associated with traditional liturgical colours, which are readily recognisable. For example,

122 Cited by Mahnke, Ibid, p.59

123 Ibid, p.59.

124 Brent Berlin and Paul Kay, <u>Basic Colour Terms; their universality and evolution</u> (Berkeley: University of California Press, 1969). Berlin and Kay carried out a number of experiments on basic colour terms. Their subjects spoke 20 different languages. This was augmented by the analysis of 78 more languages on the basis of written sources and personal contacts. Subjects were interviewed about basic colour terminology in their native language. They were then given a table of 239 colour samples and asked to match coloured chips with colours in the table.

white for light, holiness, hope, innocence, surrender, and purity; *purple* for exclusiveness, spirituality, wealth, confidence, trust, seductiveness, and secrecy; *green* for tranquillity, naturalness, growth, freshness, and resurrection; and *red* for blood, passion, life, sacrifice, love, and sensuality.

Associated with these connotations are measurable physiological responses. *Red* raises blood pressure and increases in heart and respiratory rates. Colours in the red wavelengths focus behind the retina, causing the lens adjust to a convex shape in order to draw the red light waves forward. This creates the illusion of red surfaces as closer or larger. Where *purple* is at the blue wavelength region (opposed to red) the light waves focus to the front of the retina. Here the lens flattens to make the blue surface recede and reduce in size, evoking a calming response linked to lowered heart-rate, respiration and blood pressure. *Green* light waves focus directly on the retina and are therefore experienced as restful (cool blues and greens are often used in health and healing environments). Despite its many positive connotations, *white*, says Mahnke, ranks low in colour preference tests. Questioning its use in interiors, he states that from a psychological standpoint it is sterile, effecting no psychotherapeutic benefit: "It makes us think of unemotional clinical practice rather than involved human caring. Life is colour – not detachment"[125].

Used on interior surfaces, colour, according to Mahnke, will influence a room's character differently depending on whether it is used on the floor, walls or ceiling. His summaries for the liturgical colours are of interest for the worshipping community:

---

125 Mahnke, Colour, Environment and Human Response, p.65.

Red

Ceiling: intruding, disturbing, heavy

Walls: aggressive, advancing

Floor: conscious, alert, perhaps pompous

In practical situations, pure red is seldom used as the dominant colour (on walls), but more as an accent. Although psychological arousal may be temporary, red psychologically exhibits emphatic characteristics, as discussed above. Therefore, the overuse of saturated red adds to the complexity within a space. Modifications of pure red are much more suitable.

Green

Ceiling: protective (reflection on the skin can be unattractive)

Walls: cool, secure, calm, reliable, passive, irritating if glaring (electric green), muddy if toward olive.

Floor: natural (up to a certain saturation point), soft, relaxing, cold (if toward blue-green)

Green, along with blue-green, provides a good background environment for meditation and tasks involving concentration.

Purple-Violet

Seldom used in interior spaces except for accents or special moods. Psychologically, it may appear disconcerting and subduing.

White

Ceiling: empty, no design objections – helps to diffuse light sources and reduce shadows.

Walls: neutral to empty, sterile, without energy.

Floor: touch-inhibiting (not to be walked upon).

There are psychological and physiological justifications for not using white or off-white as a dominant colour in the majority of settings.[126]

An issue for many worshipping communities is room temperature. Mahnke reports studies that demonstrate a difference of as much as 5-7°F in the subjective feeling of heat or cold between rooms painted blue-green and red-orange[127]. Also affected by colour are perception of room volume (dark or more saturated hues and/or low illumination will decrease apparent size, and vice versa); perception of weight (darker ceilings will seem lower, and low ceilings painted lighter will seem higher); perception of noise (warm and strong colours evoke loudness and vice versa - usefully exploited to compensate for noisy environments); and perception of odour and taste (used ergonomically in industrial settings to compensate for invasive odour).

There can be little doubt that the colour and quality of available light in the worship environment will profoundly influence how participants experience the space, and, therefore, in what way they will consciously or unconsciously interact with it. Choices about the sources of light are of particular importance.

---

126 Ibid, p.67-70.

127 Studies cited by Mahnke include: J.Itten, The Art of Colour (New York: Reinhold Publications, 1961),
L.A.Clark, The Ancient Art of Colour Therapy (Old Greenwich CT: Deving-Adair, 1975),
T.Porter & B.Mikellides, Colour for Architecture (New York: Van Nostrand Reinhold, 1976).

Natural light and the body

> When we speak about health, balance and physiological regulation, we are referring to the function of the body's major health keepers; the nervous system and the endocrine system. These major control centres of the body are directly stimulated and regulated by light, to an extent far beyond what modern science, until recently, has been willing to accept. *Jacob Liberman*[128]

A worshipping community which is committed to whole-body experience will be concerned with the effect of light on the well-being of the body. It is solar energy that makes life possible, and its broad band of wavelengths meets different needs and purposes. The physics of this sustaining energy were unknown to the writer of John's Gospel when he linked light and life, but the appeal to its effects were appropriately comprehensive in scope. The physiological effects of light fall into two categories: those which influence the endocrine (hormone and metabolic) system through the retina, and those resulting from light on the skin (Ott, 1982[129]). Mahnke admits that whilst there are ongoing scientific controversies about the measurable nature of the human biology of light, it would be wrong to ignore body functions which have evolved in response to the planetary cycles of solar and axis rotation. The best observed of these are the regulation of circadian rhythms (metabolic, glandular and sleep patterns) and the related production of melatonin, the hormone provided by the pineal gland to regulate the activity of several glands.

---

128 Jacob Liberman, Light: Medicine of the Future (Santa Fe: Bear & Co Publishing, 1991), p.22.

129 J.N.Ott, Light, Radiation and You (Greenwich, CT: Devin-Adair Publishers, 1982,1990)

The embodied worshipping community should, by definition, be a community of those who walk in the material as well as the immaterial light of God. This would imply a commitment to the physical qualities and pattern of daylighting, as far as possible. Daylight, the ideal full-spectrum light source provides continually changing values, brightness and contrasts, allowing the eye to adjust naturally. Short- and long-range exterior views allow the eye to change its focus (literally and metaphorically) and provide connections to the outside world of context and time. Natural light is the best source for true colour rendering and assists with the visual problems associated with ageing (which include slower adaptation to light level changes and therefore increased difficulty with glare (Edwards and Torcellini, 2002[130]).

Appealing to the Johanine partnering of light with life, I would argue that the worshipping community's arrangement of designated space should include careful consideration of the extent and quality of daylight versus artificial light.

A word about artificial light

Until the industrial revolution, people generally spent most of their time outdoors, or within close proximity to daylight. Before the 1940s, daylight was the primary light source in most buildings and artificial light was intended as supplementary. Over the next twenty years, in the developed world, human experience was transformed by the provision of ubiquitous

---

130 L.Edwards and P.Torcellini, A Literature Review of the Effects of Natural Light on Building Occupants (Colorado: National Renewable Energy Laboratory, TP-550-30769, July 2002).

artificial light. Indeed, a study by Savides et. al.[131] in the 1980s revealed average exposure to beneficial levels of daylight in the United States at only ninety minutes per day.

For most of human history the combustion of solid fuel, oil, wax or gas has provided artificial light. Glowing particles of carbon produce light that resembles the continuous spectrum of sunlight. Until recently, therefore, human experience was of artificial light that mimicked the dim natural light of sunrise and sunset, which is characteristically warm and golden in hue. As Birren points out, this artificial light was an extension of the natural pattern of daylight and darkness, and can be contrasted with the unnatural appearance of more powerful artificial sources :

> As daylight reaches higher levels, it shifts in tint from pink, to orange, to yellow, and finally into white or even blue, as from a north sky in summer. Throughout these shifts in hue, as the light level rises, the colours of objects continue to look normal. That is, no person will find the changing scene to be at all unnatural. In effect, white or daylight illumination at low levels will cast an eerie and altogether weird pallor over the world – while warm light at the same low levels will seem wholly proper[132].

The second half of the nineteenth century saw the development of the incandescent gas mantle – a material which glows by heating, requiring flame only to produce the required temperature. In the 1930s the gas light

---

131 T.J.Savides, S.Messin, C.Senger, D.F.Kripke, Natural light exposure of young adults (in Physiology and Behavior, 38(4), Oct 1986), p.571-574.

132 Faber Birren, Light, Colour and Environment, p.42.

had been almost completely replaced by electric sources. These fall into two main categories: 'incandescent' and 'discharge' lamps.

The incandescent lamp (the typical household light bulb) heats a tungsten element to incandescence within an inert gas atmosphere. Much of the emission, however, is outside the visible spectrum and falls into heat-producing infra-red region (with very little ultra violet radiation) so although cheap to produce, these lamps are relatively inefficient. Incandescent lamps produce a colour temperature which is weighted misleadingly at the warm end of the spectrum. A recent development has been the introduction of tungsten-halogen lamps which operate at a higher filament temperature. Compared with conventional incandescent lamps the halogen lamp gives a whiter light (due to higher operating temperature) and produces excellent colour-rendering properties. It's small size and longer lamp life gives it practical advantages.

Discharge lamps include all forms of fluorescent lamps, mercury or sodium discharge lamps and metal halide lamps. The light is produced by exciting gases or metal vapours by applying voltage between two electrodes is a tube filled with inert gases or metal vapours. The light becomes visible by means of a phosphor coating of the glass tube which absorbs the UV radiation and emits visible radiation due to the phenomenon of luminescence (fluorescence). The nature of the light produced is dependent on the gas used and its pressure.

Fluorescent tubes are low-pressure mercury discharge lamps which produce radiation mainly in the ultra-violet region. The majority of public buildings and work places use fluorescent lamps as their main light source, because they are cheaper, four times as efficient and last about ten times as long. The economic advantages diminish with the use of the warmer or natural light fluorescent tubes now available, but which are less efficient. Common problems associated with fluorescent sources include user complaints about glare (large exposed lamp which needs diffused), flicker, UV radiation (some is emitted, especially as tubes get older, a potential hazard for eyes and skin in the long term), and microwave radiation. Studies from the United States have shown behaviour changes in children depending on exposure to microwave and radio frequency radiation[133].

Some priorities for the use of material light in the worship environment

1. Intentionality

The carefully planned and embodied worship environment requires the intentional use of light and colour. Arrangements for natural and artificial illumination, as well as the colours of the surfaces reflecting that light, should be an integral part of the community's engagement with space as sacred. Attending to these foundational elements of visual experience can never be afterthoughts (retro-fitted for utilitarian reasons). In the same way, if the worship of the community is to be an outpouring of the dynamic, common life of a changing, organic and embodied people, then the provision of light and colour created for the worship of a previous generation will not generally suffice. The subject must never be ignored or dismissed as secondary. As Boyce puts it:

---

133 For a more detailed discussion see London Hazards Centre Trust, Fluorescent Lighting (London Hazards Centre Trust Ltd, March 1987).

Lighting does more than just make things visible. Lighting in a space inevitably contributes to people's impressions of the space. The impression may be good or bad, appropriate or inappropriate, firm or vague, but it will exist. There are positive and negative aspects to the influence of lighting on impression. The negative aspect is dominant when there are complaints of discomfort. The positive aspects are apparent when feelings of pleasure are experienced. But discomfort and pleasure are not the only possible impressions lighting can give. It is much more complicated than that. Lighting can give an interior a character. This character may be dramatic, inviting, depressing, boring, relaxing, interesting, functional, etc. It is the subtlety of the various impressions that can be evoked and the practicality of doing so that makes lighting such an important means of manipulation.[134]

The lighting designer William Lam defines light as the "principal medium" which puts people in touch with their environment. The provision of artificial light has, he says, been surrendered to "building owners with misconceived programmatic objectives, and to misguided government officials, who have been brainwashed by propaganda from the lighting and power industry into adopting and enforcing irrelevant and obstructive codes in the name of progress"[135]. Although luminance levels are vital for "activity needs", the overall quality of the environment will be determined, he says, by patterns of light sources and their relationship to the visual field. A walk into the bright and inspiring atmosphere of a Baroque church or the inviting

134 P.R.Boyce, Human Factors in Lighting (London: Applied Science Publishers, 1981), p.255.
135 William C.Lam, Perception and Lighting as Formgivers for Architecture (New York: McGraw-Hill, 1977), p.10.

corners of a sophisticated restaurant provide obvious examples of the effects light can have in interior spaces. By contrast, as a direct outcome of the neglect of whole-body experience, the lighting of worship environments has too often been oriented to 'task', often the only criterion applied.

2. Patterns and shadows

Alexander (et al)[136], from the Centre for Environmental Structure in California, argue that 'patterns' provide the architectural language of human-oriented design. Among these are patterns of light. In interiors with uniform light levels there are no 'places' which can provide contexts for human events. Such places are usually defined by light. People are, they say, 'phototropic' by nature in that they move towards light, and when stationary, orient themselves toward the light (this defines the appeal of window seats, verandas, and fireside corners – "places where things happen"). Thus, "if places where the light falls are not the places you are meant to go toward, or if the light is uniform, the environment is giving information which contradicts its own meaning"[137]. Elsewhere, in the description of another pattern, "pools of light", uniform lighting is described as the "sweetheart of the lighting engineer...[which] serves no useful purpose whatsoever. In fact it destroys the social nature of space and makes people feel disorientated and unbounded"[138]. The potential implications for worship communities and their ritual events are obvious enough, and more will be said later about the shaping of space for worship.

136 Christopher Alexander, et al, A Pattern Language (New York: Oxford University Press, 1977).

137 Ibid, p.646.

138 Ibid, p.1160.

Patterns of light are, by definition, dependent on the relationship of light and shadow. This relationship is the building material of the shape of space. As we instinctively use shadow that is both 'attached' (surfaces of an object that are away from the light) and 'cast' (created by an object between us and the light), we glean impressive amounts of information about gradient and surface. In its weave of contrast and layer lie the visual clues to depth, distance, direction and priority. Michel[139] describes this as the "animation" of the human environment, where texture enlivens surfaces by the introduction of shadow. There are, he says, human responses to rhythm which should be exploited in the composition of light and shade.

Shadow is to be distinguished from darkness, since it comprises a plethora of levels of coloured light of varying intensity and, like light in its material form, should be liberated from its metaphorical association with ignorance, sin and death. There are no simple shadows. Those cast by 'point' sources of light (a bright single source, like a spotlight) will be darker, with sharp edges. This area (the 'umbra') is totally hidden from the point source. Extended sources of light, like the sun, cast both an umbra and a 'penumbra' – a softer, and variable quality of shadow.

Interiors will typically feature a combination of light sources (which themselves will vary immensely between day and night conditions) and the interplay of shadows can be manipulated by suitable additions or subtractions, as well as by the arrangement of objects. The colour of shadow will depend on the colour of the light shining into it, the intrinsic colour of the object on which the shadow is cast, and the psychological factor of chromatic adaptation. In his 1933 essay, "In Praise of Shadows", the novelist

139 Lou Michel, Light: The Shape of Space , p.5.

Tanizaki celebrates the traditional Japanese aesthetic of subdued interiors and argues for its preservation in the face of encroaching Westernised commitment to ever brighter illumination. Beauty, he says, "must always grow from the realities of life, and our ancestors, forced to live in dark rooms, presently came to discover beauty in shadows, ultimately to guide shadows towards beauty's ends."[140] For Tanizaki there is a sacredness about the beauty found in the sculpture of shadow against shadow, and the use of material and colours that respond mysteriously to fragile light (as in the impalpable, faltering candle flame collecting in pools against lacquerware or gold leaf). In contrast, the "progressive Westerner", he says, "spares no pains to eradicate even the mutest shadow"[141].

In his critique of the ocular bias in architecture, Pallusmaa refers to the concerns of Walter Ong in identifying the eye as the organ of distance and separation which surveys and controls . Engagement with the quality of light and shadow, he says, is how whole-body experience can be liberated:

> The imagination and daydreaming are stimulated by dim light and shadow. In order to think clearly, the sharpness of vision has to be suppressed, for thoughts travel with an absent-minded and unfocused gaze. Homogeneous bright light paralyses the imagination in the same way that homogenisation of space weakens the experience of being and wipes away the sense of space. The human eye is most perfectly tuned for twilight rather than bright daylight... The shadow gives shape and life to the object in light. It also provides the realm from which fantasies and dreams arise... In

---

140 Junichirō Tanizaki, <u>In Praise of Shadows</u> (London: Vintage, 2001), p.29.
141 Ibid, p.48.

great architectural spaces there is a constant, deep breathing of shadow and light; shadow inhales and illumination exhales light.[142]

With a reminder that constant bright illumination is used as a form of torture, Pallasmaa notes that states of affectivity and emotion are associated with a shift from vision to the other senses, and from light to shadow (most obviously in the case of lovers who want nothing to detract from the intensity of their shared intimacy). By contrast, a culture or institution which seeks control over the users of its space (a manufacturing utility, an open plan office, or a church?) "is likely to promote the opposite direction of interaction, away from intimate individuality and identification towards a public and distant detachment"[143].

To celebrate material light in the worship environment will involve the creative interplay of light and shadow at the expense of bright, uniform illumination. As the photographer seeks out drama and strength in the contrast and pattern of a side-lit portrait or sun-lit landscape (flood/flash lighting or monochromatic skies are more obviously uninspiring here), whole-body experience in the illumined, community gathering place calls for careful composition.

Whole-body experience and unfocused vision

For Pallasmaa, architecture has been diminished by a bias towards 'focused' vision. Physical space is not experienced as a series of retinal images but "in

---

142 Juhani Pallasmaa, The Eyes of the Skin: Architecture and the Senses (Chichester: Wiley, 2005), pp.46-47.

143 Ibid, p.49.

its integrated material, embodied and spiritual essence"[144]. In a way that again recalls Ong's contrast of oral and visual culture, Pallasmaa says that focused vision confronts us with the world and sets us apart from it. This, in turn, has led to a de-emphasis of sensory or affective qualities in buildings and the spaces they provide. What is needed, he says, is a recovery of the importance of 'unfocused' or peripheral vision, which "envelops us in the flesh of the world":

> A remarkable factor in the experiencing of enveloping spatiality, interiority and hapticity is the deliberate suppression of sharp, focused vision. This issue has hardly entered the theoretical discourse of architecture as architectural theorising continues to be interested in focused vision, conscious intentionality and perspectival representation. Photographed architectural images are centralised images of focused gestalt; yet the quality of an architectural reality seems to depend fundamentally on the nature of peripheral vision, which enfolds the subject in the space. A forest context, and richly moulded architectural space, provide ample stimuli for peripheral vision, and these settings centre us in the very space. The preconscious perceptual realm, which is experienced outside the sphere of focused vision, seems to be just as important existentially as the focused image. In fact, there is medical evidence that peripheral vision has a higher priority in our perceptual and mental system.

These observations suggest that one of the reasons why the architectural and urban settings of our time tend to make us feel like

---

144 Ibid, p.11.

outsiders, in comparison with the forceful emotional engagement of natural and historical settings, is their poverty in the field of peripheral vision. Unconscious peripheral perception transforms retinal gestalt into spatial and bodily experiences. Peripheral vision integrates us with space, while focused vision pushes us out of the space, making us mere spectators. The defensive and unfocused gaze of our time, burdened by sensory overload, may eventually open up new realms of vision and thought, freed of the implicit desire of the eye for control and power. The loss of focus can liberate the eye from its historical patriarchal domination.[145]

This is an important contribution to the conception of an embodied environment for the worshipping community. Visual experience of material light is to be understood as part of the whole-body dynamic that constitutes 'being in the world'. To arrange a space for worship is to allow for an arena that, in Pallasmaa's words, addresses all the senses simultaneously and fuses our image of self with our experience of the world: "The world is reflected in the body, and the body is projected onto the world. We remember through our bodies as much as through our nervous system and brain"[146]. An embodied approach which takes account of the physiological and psychological effects of material light in the arrangement of the unconscious, unfocused and peripheral visual environment is, I would argue, an implied demand of a theology of the body.

---

145 Ibid, p.12.

146 Ibid, p.45.

94

Screens in church – a short digression

One practical implication of the appeal to unfocused vision may be to critique the increased use of large-format projection screens in worship environments. In his own critique of computer imaging in architectural design, Pallasmaa argues that it deconstructs the multi-sensory and synchronic capacity for imagination and locates the process in the realms of passive visual manipulation and retinal journey.

Heralded as liberators of book-bound, liturgically-controlled and paper-swamped worshippers everywhere, projection screens, in my view, similarly belong to the apparatus of control. The effect is to rein in embodied worship experience in favour of a more regulated, ocular religious form. The screen creates distance between the participant and the object (language or image) in much the way Walter Ong describes the objectivising of the written word.

By contrast, to physically participate in the worship space (or its creation) by means of whole-body experience, puts the worshipper into a haptic relationship with the process. Even when engaging with the written word, to handle a book or printed sheet is to make decisions about which page or paragraph to look at or dwell on, with an object that the individual can touch, manipulate, write on, mask, tear, fold or share. As they age, a liturgy or song book and the experience they evoke are located firmly in time. Unlike the ephemeral projected image, they can be ignored or forever treasured.

Conclusion

Inspired or hindered by the ubiquitous divinisation of immaterial light, the visual experience of the embodied worshipper is a complex response to the effects of material light, and is to be celebrated as part of whole-body encounter with the worship environment. Isolation of the eye from its proper interaction with other biological and psychological processes of perception (because of the prioritising of focused vision) denies the complexity of the perceptual system and creates potential for detachment and alienation.

Chapter Four

Auditory experience in the worship environment. The physical and psychophysical effects of sound and of making music.

Introduction

> The hearing ear and the seeing eye – the Lord has made them both. *Proverbs 20:12*

> Morning by morning he wakens – wakens my ear to listen as those who are taught. *Isaiah 50: 4*

> Let anyone with ears listen! *Matthew 11: 15*

> The reason I speak to them in parables is that "seeing they do not perceive, and hearing they do not listen, nor do they understand".
> With them indeed is fulfilled the prophecy of Isaiah that says:
> "You will indeed listen, but never understand,
> and you will indeed look, but never perceive.
> For this people's heart has grown dull,
> and their ears are hard of hearing,
> and they have shut their eyes;
> so that they might not look with their eyes,
> and listen with their ears,
> and understand with their heart and turn -
> and I would heal them".

> But blessed are your eyes, for they see, and your ears, for they hear.
>
> *Matthew 13:13ff*

The obvious interpretation of this kind of biblical material is that aural (as well as visual) language is used principally as a metaphor for religious knowledge or gnosis. 'To hear' and 'to be heard' are metaphors for spiritual understanding, obedience and attentiveness to divine instruction. The Old Testament is strewn with prophetic and psalmic appeals to hear God's promises and judgements, and for supplications and offerings of worship to be heard by God. In turn, Jesus describes the spiritual and moral shortcomings of his generation in terms of blindness and deafness. As we have seen, to interpret such sensory language as purely gnostic metaphor, particularly in our conception of physically-located worship practice, is to risk the dismantling of whole-body experience.

The broader view is that an embodied understanding of seeing and hearing includes a commitment to engage with sensory awareness as the conduit of spiritual discovery, the basis of affective worship practice and, consequently, of the ordering of worship environments. In this view, the members of the worshipping community will authentically see and hear the implications of their devotions insofar as their whole bodies are involved in the experience. This chapter will argue for a whole-body appreciation of auditory experience, with reference to the psycho-physics of sound and of song.

> The embryo consists of three layers, which will later become the human body. They are the endoderm, the mesoderm and the ectoderm. The ectoderm will develop into the skin, the ear and the nervous system. The fact that the nervous system stems from the same origin as the ear and the skin is a subject for further meditation when thinking about the meaning and role of music in human development.[147]

When we ask someone to listen, we are requiring them to attend consciously to an immensely complex psychophysical process which, for the most part, continues without interruption in the realm of the unconscious. 'Psycho-acoustics' is the auditory extension of the study of sensory responses to physical stimuli. The stimuli in this case, what we call sound, are the pulsating movements of air molecules caused by the mechanical movement of objects, however large or small. These waves, which ripple out in every direction, travel at 1100 feet per second (compared with light's 186,000 miles per second) reflecting off the variety of surfaces at hand and causing the eardrum to vibrate. Only extremely small levels of sound-wave pressure are needed to stimulate the ear drum, which moves the tiny middle ear bones; the 'hammer', 'anvil' and 'stirrup' – the smallest bones in the body. These in turn connect to another membrane, the 'oval window', which is the point of transfer to the inner ear, the 'cochlea', which consists of three fluid filled chambers. Along one side of the cochlea is the 'basilear membrane' and its movements are sensed by hair cells (collectively known as the 'organ of Corti') which function as transducers, converting mechanical energy to

---

147 Paul Madaule, Listening and Singing (in NATS Journal of Singing: Jacksonville FL May/June 2001), p.8.

electromagnetic energy. This makes possible the transfer of auditory signals to the perception processes of the brain.

Emphasising the association of the embodied listener with the physical environment, Diane Ackerman points out that this process "bridges the ancient barrier between air and water, taking sound waves, translating them into fluid waves, and then into electrical impulses[148]". At its best, the human auditory system can detect frequencies in the range between 16 and 20,000 cycles per second (with age, the ear drum thickens and higher frequencies transfer less efficiently) and responds across a vast range of intensity. For a detailed account of the physiology of the ear see, Moore, 1989[149]; Radocy and Boyle, 2003[150]; Handel, 1989[151].

Sophisticated perceptive abilities allow for the capability of distinguishing loudness and intensity. According to Handel, the difference in loudness between the system's detection threshold to that of pain is about 150 decibels (a ratio of about 30 million to 1). The complexity of the interpretative interplay between the listener and the environment is of particular importance. As Ackerman puts it:

> At a busy cocktail party in a room with a low ceiling and poor acoustics, sound waves hit the wall and bounce back rather than being absorbed, and you feel as if you're in the centre of a handball court in the middle of a game. Yet you can slice through all the noise

148 Diane Ackerman, A Natural History of the Senses (London: Phoenix, 1996), p.178.

149 B.C.J.Moore, An introduction to the psychology of hearing (San Diego/London: Academic Press, 1997).

150 R.E.Radocy and J.D.Boyle, Psychological Foundations of Musical Behaviour (Illinois: Thomas, 2003).

151 Stephen Handel, Listening: An Introduction to the Perception of Auditory Events (Cambridge, Mass: MIT Press, 1989), p.461ff.

to hear one conversation taking place between your spouse and a flirtatious stranger.[152]

As we shall see, the musician's perspective might well be to disagree with Ackerman's view on the merits of a reverberant acoustic, but the ability to 'sort out' auditory information, notably beyond the scope of most hearing aids, assumes proper importance with an appreciation of the complexities of reflected sound in the environment.

Resonance in the environment and in the body

The ways in which sound waves are reflected and scattered by the objects and surfaces in a given environment is critical to aural experience. A commitment to whole-body experience in the worship space includes an appreciation of the fact that sounds arriving at the ear are not the same as those that left their source. As Handel explains:

> The environment may generate multiple representations of a single source because of reflection; it may generate a modified spectrum and a modified spatial distribution because of interference from the objects and resonances of an enclosure. In addition, the body itself acts to alter and reflect the sound reaching the listener's ears, and movement of the source or the listener acts to alter the sound in still different ways. The role of the environment is ambiguous. In one way it introduces error and uncertainty by bringing about changes in

152 Ackerman, A Natural History of the Senses, p.181.

the acoustic wave. In another way it aids perceiving by creating multiple yet modified signals that can be related and compared to each other to recover the original signal.[153]

Capacious church buildings are renowned for their elaborate acoustic qualities, where the listener is subjected to a long sequence of sound waves arriving at different times. The length and quality of the reverberation will depend on the number and distance of reflecting surfaces and the effect may be experienced as pleasing or destructive, depending on the context. A long, sonorous acoustic may enhance the sound of a solo singing voice, but be catastrophic for oratory or large-group conversation.

Perception of sound is closely related to the physical environment, because enclosed spaces impose their particular resonant qualities. An individual enclosed space provides unique characteristics of resonance and reverberation, and any sound introduced into it, whose frequency is close to a characteristic resonance of the space, will be enhanced with the sympathetic vibration of the air. In the worship context this can, for example, provide a partial explanation as to why corporate song in a given location, with a given set of voices, arranged in a given physical formation, may evoke a noticeably exhilarating or emotive experience for those who are singing or listening. The resonating and reverberating environment for worship can be manipulated and exploited (by design, by retro-fit or re-ordering) so as to suit the intended purposes of its users. The most obvious examples would be to use reverberant or resonant spaces for singing, and a controlled, absorbent acoustic for small group discussion.

---

153 Handel, Listening, p.79.

These dynamics become familiar to us as the characteristic acoustic of a given space, because its resonant spectrum will consistently reinforce or neglect particular frequencies. However, an embodied use of aural space demands an acknowledgement of the body as a resonant and mobile predictable presence within it.

The body as a resonator

Embryologists generally agree that the ear is the first organ in the embryo to develop, that it begins functioning at eighteen weeks and 'listens actively' by twenty-four weeks[154]. Sound, therefore, is the first functioning mode of perception. Because amniotic fluid fills the nose and mouth and suspends the body, the foetus, according to Verney[155], has no sense of sight, smell or touch. Throughout its development, therefore, it lives in an environment of heightened sound, with vibration as its principal sense. According to musicologist Maconie: "In infancy our understanding of the world develops as a cooperative relationship of aural and visual perceptions, of which hearing is initially the superior sense, because it comes ready-made and fully functioning, whereas seeing has to be learned"[156].

The argument for the bodily primacy of the auditory realm is furthered by the physical definition of each cell of the body being in constant motion or vibration, with associated sympathetic resonances. This is a view of the body as a resonant cavity, awash with internal reflections and vibrations coming

154 Thomas Verney, The Secret Life of the Unborn Child (New York: Dell, 1981), p.38.
155 Ibid, p.38.
156 Robin Maconie, The Science of Music (Oxford: Clarendon Press, 1997), p.xii.

from many oscillators such as organs, tissues, cells and molecules. This principle is the basis of music and vibration therapies which seek to harmonise the body's resonances internally and with the outside world. Wigram[157] expansively reviews research into the physical and psychological effects of vibration in the clinical (vibro-acoustic therapy) and occupational realms – for example, the potential hazards of man-made low-frequency noise and, in particular, infrasonic noise that is below the audible range:

> Parts of the body, particularly cavities, which contain different kinds of gasses or air, such as the lungs, the intestines, the stomach, the ear and the nose are more sensitive to infrasound than parts which are homogeneous and which do not contain gasses.[158]

Typically, says Wigram, even low levels of infrasound are found to affect the working environment and alter efficiency, alertness and physical behaviour. High 'ultrasonic' frequencies are familiar from their medical uses, mostly in diagnostic imaging, whilst high-frequency vibration of muscular tissue is commonly used in physiotherapy.

The effects of inaudible frequencies are traditionally associated with meditative states. The mantras and chants of many religious traditions are commonly believed to have a profoundly calming effect, just as some associated musical instruments (such as Tibetan thigh bone trumpets) resonate at the same frequency as some parts of the human body. Tibetan singing bowls are similarly thought to stimulate specific frequencies in the brain and such ancient technology may be expressed in the design of ritual

157Anthony Wigram, The Effects of Vibroacoustic Therapy on Clinical and Non-Clinical Populations, (Unpublished PhD Research Thesis, St George's Hospital, London University.
158 Ibid, p.55

buildings (tombs, burial chambers, cathedrals and temples) which amplify or modulate the resonances of rhythmic chants, singing or music.

Archaeologist Aaron Watson of Reading University has led a series of studies into the acoustic properties of Neolithic monuments in the United Kingdom and Ireland. Watson argues that although scholars have focused on the visual aspects of these sites (how their form, location and alignment contribute to ceremonial use), sound may also have played an important role. The internal structure and layout of tombs like Maes Howe in Orkney demonstrates apparently intentional acoustic effects, one of which is the recorded phenomenon known as a 'standing wave', produced when two sound waves of equal frequency and intensity travel in opposing directions. This can produce distinct areas of low or high intensity as the sound waves interact, sometimes cancelling each other out or combining to enhance the sound. Watson's suggestion is that infrasonic vibrations created within the tombs could have been used to alter the mental states of those participating in ceremonies. Another acoustic property that seems to be associated with the tombs is the principle of 'Helmholtz Resonance', similar to the phenomenon produced by blowing across the neck of a bottle. Passage graves such as Maes Howe and bottles share the same basic structure: a chamber connected to the outside world by a long, narrow neck. To create this effect, the tomb users would have had to create a sound within the chamber that was at precisely the correct pitch for the dimensions and design of the chamber. The larger the chamber, the lower the pitch required to create the resonance effect. At Maes Howe, for example, researchers found that the correct pitch, produced by a drum, was of infrasonic frequency.

Although inaudible to the human auditory system, such frequencies can be felt as distinct physical or psychological sensations. Watson suggests that these acoustic effects were deliberate and marked the tombs as spiritually significant places:

> How, then, could people in the Neolithic generate Helmholtz Resonance? Interestingly, acoustic physics suggests that these low frequencies could best have been initiated by performing rhythmical drumming in the chamber, with the speed of the beat relating to the size of the tomb. Camster Round, for example, resonates at a frequency of 4 hertz, which could be produced by drumming at the rate of four beats per second. Maes Howe resonates at 2 hertz, or by drumming at two beats per second.
>
> Drumming has accompanied ritual in many societies through time and it is not impossible that it was employed in prehistoric Britain. Perhaps we can envisage entering the darkened environment of the chamber where the stale air, peculiar smells, and presence of the dead would heighten the senses to any sounds being made. Combined with echoes and possibly resonance, these elements could have amounted to a remarkable and affecting experience.[159]

Contemporary demonstrations of this phenomenon are easily found. The physical impact of high intensity, rhythmic-based music is at the core of club culture, where the combination of sustained bodily exertion and enclosed space, literally throbbing with a broad spectrum of resonant frequencies (the most favoured of which are subsonic), is used to effect some degree of

---

159 Aaron Watson, Hearing Again the Sound of the Neolithic (in British Archaeology, 23, April 1997).

consciousness-altering experience, often enhanced by the effects of alcohol or recreational drugs. Significantly, this deeply embodied form of recreation lies at the heart of the leisure and entertainment industry. No self-respecting cinema would be without sophisticated surround-sound systems which physically cause the environment and the seats to resonate in ways that are seen as vital to the emotional impact of the storyline. Quite apart from their visual manipulations, cinematic soundtracks are carefully contrived to impose auditory experience that goes far beyond naturalistic reality in their quest to locate the affective experience of the audience. Increasingly used in home entertainment systems, sound is used to enhance the illusion that the viewer is 'in the middle' of the action, and to physically feel the weight of every collision or punch. Computer game pads vibrate in the players' hands in an attempt to reconnect the detached visual graphics with bodily experience.

The principle is no less present in the more controlled environments of choral and orchestral music or, I would argue, in the impact of powerful organ music which is used to provide the physical experience of resonance in so many worship spaces, as anyone who has sat in the choir stalls beneath a great cathedral organ will testify. Contemporary worship forms using rock or club idioms and powerful sound systems introduce resonant encounter in the same way.

My proposition is that body resonances account for at least some of what contemporary worshippers experience as affective religious feelings or emotions, and that this is to be celebrated and explored in authentic whole-body ritual. However, the appeal here is not for louder organs, or the effects of infrasonic drum sounds and sound systems. Passive resonant experience is not only the poorer cousin, but all too often also the suppressor of active, participatory experience. I would advocate the prioritisation of what is arguably the most embodied of sensory experience – corporate song.

Resonant singing and the ear of the body

A glance at the Old Testament shows that the ancient Hebrews were committed to the use of music, which maintains a central place in the historical, prophetic and wisdom literature. Every aspect of human experience is represented in the wealth of songs and psalms of a people who incorporated them seamlessly into their model of divine service. During the exilic period, faced with losing their songs (and therefore their identity) scribes translated and paraphrased Hebrew songs and scriptures into Aramaic. This became known as the Targum, meaning 'the translation'. The inclusion of some of this material in the Old Testament signifies the importance of these songs in the memory and worship of the Hebrews. For an overview of the songs of Moses, the Psalter, Luke's Gospel, and Revelation, see Lockyer, 2004[160]. If the history of the Christian church is inextricably linked with song, there is, a considerable danger that the church has forgotten the reasons why.

Trained singers know that the whole body is involved in the act of singing. In order to master fine tuning and control, they are taught to nurture the ability to listen to their own voice. This listening is, according to Madaule, "a primary sensory experience that involves both the ear and the body.

160 Herbert Lockyer, All The Music of the Bible (Peabody Mass: Hendrickson Publishers Inc, 2004).

Listening to oneself sing begins the moment the larynx vibrates and triggers bone conduction"[161]. Referring to the work of the renowned singing teacher Alfred Tomatis[162], Madaule argues that singing is best understood by those who listen with the kinaesthetic and tactile process of bodily experience:

> Tomatis views audio-vocal control as a two-step process. In the first step, vibration of the larynx is transmitted via the spine to the bone structure of the body and to the inner ear by bone conduction. The purpose of this first short ear-voice feedback loop is to alert the brain that a sound, in need of being properly shaped by the vocal tract, is on its way. Bone-conducted audio-vocal control gives the singer the kinaesthetic awareness – or "feeling" – of his or her voice. It gives the sense of connecting with one's voice. At the same time, this triggering of the vibration of the bony shell surrounding the resonating cavities of the head and chest enriches the resonance of the sound. In the second step of the audio-vocal control, the sound travels through the vocal tract out of the mouth and is picked up by the ear via air conduction. The time lapse between these two steps (bone and air conduction) gives the singer the time to adjust the position, tension and shape of the many parts of the body involved in the act of singing.... The sound vibration generated by the body is transmitted through the surrounding space, making the room an extended resonating cavity that becomes an integral part of the singer's voice.[163]

161 Madaule, Listening and Singing, p.5.

162 Alfred Tomatis, The Ear and Language (Norval: Moulin Publishing, 1996) and The Conscious Ear (Barrytown: Station Hill Press, 1991).

163 Madaule, Listening and Singing, p.3.

According to Handel, approximately one hundred muscles are involved in the process of vocal production and, given the rapidity with which individual muscular events occur, the body requires to make predictive movements:

> The production system must cheat in order to get all the sounds out rapidly: movements appropriate to several successive sounds must be made simultaneously, and movements necessary to produce future sounds must be started early enough to ensure that the vocal tract will be in the correct position to make those sounds when they are required.[164]

Handel goes on to describe the body's involvement in a four part process: *airstream* (where air is expelled from the lungs); *phonation* (where air from the lungs is set into vibration); *articulatory* (where the vibration pattern is modified by the resonances of the sound body formed by the oral and nasal cavities); and *radiation* (where the vibration is radiated into the air). If singing stimulates and exercises breathing, improves posture and promotes the circulation of the blood and other fluids, it is unsurprising that so embodied a function should elicit psycho-physical responses. According to Ackerman, "our pupils dilate and our endorphin level rises when we sing; music engages the whole body, as well as the brain, and there is a healing quality to it"[165]. Comatose patients, she points out, and those with learning disabilities are commonly observed to respond emotionally to music and song, and music therapists, as part of their process, will often find it possible to encourage those unable to speak to communicate first in song.

---

164 Handel, Listening, p.134.

165 Ackerman, A Natural History of the Senses, p.217.

Cindy Bell reports the findings of a study by the U.S. National Endowment of the Arts (1997) which suggest that the most popular public arts activity in the United States is choral singing which "far outshines other arts activities such as drama, dance, painting or drawing"[166]. In addressing motivations for this phenomenon, Bell quotes the choral conductor and arranger Harry Robert Wilson:

> The person who joins a chorus is seeking, primarily, to satisfy through the medium of singing a longing for something beautiful and spiritual in his life. There may be social motives but the musical motive is invariably stronger. The most natural and at the same time the most universal medium for experiencing music is that of singing. The total physical and emotional responses in the act of singing make it the most personal musical activity. Singing also affects the entire body more directly and more intimately than any other musical experience.[167]

Unrestricted by language, singing is the most physical articulation of the body, and because of the resonance of the body, music and song which come from external sources (most recognisably the voices of others) also sound through the body. Human voices co-joined in community, say Saliers and Saliers, "are primary instruments of the soul, and thus a medium for expressing what goes beyond the immediate, common sense world. All such musical experiences help us see that hearing and sound encode more than what we hear".[168]

---

166 Cindy Bell, Community Choirs, (in International Journal of Research in Choral Singing 2(1), 2004), p.39.

167 H.R.Wilson, Artistic Choral Singing (in Journal of Research in Music Education, 37(1), p.32-47; quoted in C.Bell, Community Choirs, p.46.

We can conclude, therefore, that the worshipping community which sings well together is engaged in a most embodied interaction, with one other and with its physical environment. For these reasons, I suggest that the corporal demands of New Testament ecclesiology imply a commitment to participatory song, in terms that go beyond routinised and relatively passive hymn-singing. Singing and listening with the body, as part of whole-body ritual requires appropriate practices and environments. Dominant organ accompaniment, for example, and dispersed or mono-directional seating arrangements severely limit the potential for resonant experience. The corporate body finds it more possible to sing together affectively and emotionally than to speak together. Arguably, the best rehearsed spoken liturgy can be the least evocative as a corporate experience. The Scots hymn writer and liturgist John Bell (2000[169]) describes in detail the ways in which communal song in the worshipping community enables religious memory (oral tradition), scriptural rendition, group identity, egalitarian participation and celebrates a creative dynamic of ritual event. What he articulates is the unusually inclusive potential of community singing (where no expertise or performance skill is required) to involve participants in a corporate creative act, as they transform the written or learned idea into experience:

> When we sing we do something unique... when we sing and enliven the text through music, and enter into that music not just with our mouth and ears, but with our whole being, then we are doing something which is both personal and holistic... when these particular voices engage with their selected songs, it will be an unrepeatable event..... And so something extremely rare happens

168 D.Saliers and E.Saliers, <u>A Song To Sing, A Life To Live</u> (San Francisco: Jossey-Bass, 2005), p.35.

169 John L.Bell, <u>The Singing Thing</u> (Glasgow: Wild Goose Publications, 2000).

whenever a congregation sings to its Maker. For not only are there ten or fifty or five hundred individual voices giving their unique gift as they open their mouths and sing; there is also the unique blending of high and low voices, sharp and flat, sophisticated and rough-tongued, male and female, old and young..... if we can but sense it, every time a congregation sings, it is offering an absolutely one-time-only gift to its Maker."[170]

In conclusion, I will argue that positive commitment to such auditory aspects of whole-body experience is a prerequisite for the worshipping community if it hopes to nurture a sense of its own located being, and therein to encourage ecclesial sacredness of space.

Sound, location and community

Hearing is omnidirectional; vision is directional. Hearing is permanently in focus; vision is continually changing in focus. The sound world is intermittent and subject to decay; the visual world appears continuous and permanent. The world of hearing is necessarily dynamic; that of sight is necessarily static and apparently instantaneous. The two senses give rise to versions of reality that are not bound to coincide, and are frequently contradictory.
Robin Maconie[171]

Music forms us into communities from which we take, in large

---

170 Ibid, pp.78-80.

171 Maconie, The Science of Music, p.xii.

measure, our personal identity. Yet who we are, as individuals and as communities, is also open to the songs we have yet to hear. *Saliers and Saliers*[172]

Buildings do not react to our gaze, but they do return our sounds back to our ears. *Juhani Pallasmaa*[173]

Just as I have argued that the provision of light and colours used to shape the worship environment should never be careless or utilitarian, the whole-body approach to auditory experience is of far greater importance than whether individuals are able to hear the voice of the celebrant, the choir or the organ. A sound-sensitive approach will contribute significantly to the possibility of an experience that is 'affective' (the reference here is to Davis' concept of feeling) in locating the community in space which they consider sacred. If sanctity is located in the assembly of the believers (which, as we have seen is the prevailing biblical emphasis), then the psychophysical effects of sound presented here are directly relevant to located, sacred ritual event.

Auditory experience has an impact on located and collective experience that goes beyond that of the visual. This argument recalls Walter Ong's critique of visually dominated experience in its power to objectify the world and distance the viewer from it. For Ong, visual culture encourages us to be observers who spectate from the sidelines of our own perspective. Auditory stimuli, on the other hand, surround us. Immersed in this resonance, we unconsciously navigate sonic space, aware that we are at its centre - more 'in the world' as surrounded participants. Vision isolates, says Pallasmaa,

---

172 D.Saliers and E.Saliers, <u>A Song To Sing, A Life To Live</u>, p.83.

173 Juhani Pallasmaa, <u>The Eyes of the Skin: Architecture and the Senses</u> (Chichester: Wiley, 2005), p.49.

whereas sound incorporates: "The sense of sight implies exteriority, but sound creates an experience of interiority. I regard an object, but sound approaches me; the eye reaches, but the ear receives"[174].

Referring to this participatory dynamic, Maconie characterises aural cultures as those which exploit the mystery of unison singing. To sing in unison, he says, is "charged with mystery since it manifests the paradoxical idea that two or more bodies can occupy the same physical space" - a function which light sources or colours cannot fulfil. Instead of corrupting one other, says Maconie, unison voices co-exist, a fact "which can only be explained by postulating an alternative reality for acoustic events, a reality in which unison bodies are able to occupy the same space together"[175].

Even where not in unison, and where tones clash or create harmony, it is possible in the creation of a new sound for the constituent tones to be retained. A chord, says Ackerman, is "something like an idea" - an audible idea[176]. The collective audible idea is what creates a sense of connection, which is Pallasmaa's generic dynamic in the auditory potential of architectural interiors:

> Sight is the sense of the solitary observer, whereas hearing creates a sense of connection and solidarity; our look wanders lonesomely in the dark depths of a cathedral, but the sound of the organ makes us immediately experience our affinity with the space..... the sound reverberating from surrounding walls puts us in direct interaction

---

174 Ibid, p.49.

175 Maconie, The Science of Music, p.92.

176 Ackerman, A Natural History of the Senses, p.217.

with space; the sound measures space and makes its scale comprehensible.[177]

Architectural environments' most essential auditory function, says Pallasmaa, is tranquility. Numbed by the world's constant blanket of acoustic-deadening and background 'musak', we are unable to locate ourselves in the acoustic volume of space. The silence of architecture is, he says, a responsive, remembering silence which "emancipates us from the embrace of the present and allows us to experience the slow, healing flow of time.... matter, space and time fuse into one singular elemental experience, the sense of being"[178]. Typically available in resonant church spaces, such opportunity for collective, locative silence is too often overlooked by the worshipping community, for whom silence should also be an integral element in auditory experience.

In the remaining chapter I will argue that the interaction of the worshipping community with designated liturgical space should be understood principally as a collective ritual, whereby whole-body experience (visual, auditory and haptic) provides the community with the potential to physically constitute 'the priesthood of all believers'.

---

177 Pallasmaa, The Eyes of the Skin, p.50.

178 Ibid, p.52.

Chapter Five

Touching the void – being present to ritual event and re-membering the body

Introduction

I have proposed that the practice of the worshipping community should be understood as whole-body experience, whereby participants are involved in a continuous embodied dialogue with their environment. The community's arrangement of its designated environment is critical, since it is impossible for participants to detach their image of self from the spatial and situational event. Since the sense of reality sought after in the worship context is governed, strengthened and articulated by the ongoing sensory encounter, participation in ritual event takes place at the frontier of the body's physical and psychophysical system. In his evocative architectural polemic, Pallasmaa chooses some ecclesiastical imagery:

> ....my legs measure the length of the arcade and the width of the square; my gaze unconsciously projects my body onto the façade of the cathedral, where it roams over the mouldings and contours, sensing the size of the recesses and projections; my body weight meets the mass of the cathedral door, and my hand grasps the doorpull as I enter the dark void behind.... The city and my body supplement and define each other. I dwell in the city and the city dwells in me.[179]

---

179 Juhani Pallasmaa, The Eyes of the Skin, p. 40.

Good architecture and, by definition therefore, good environments for worship will enhance the experience of self. What is striking about Pallasmaa's ideal is the potential for bodily *participation* in the environment. In his pioneering work on perception, J.J.Gibson[180] characterises the senses as 'aggressively seeking mechanisms' rather than passive receivers. They can be categorised into five participatory sensory systems: the visual; the auditory; the taste-smell; the basic-orienting; and the haptic. Having considered the visual and auditory realms, I want to take further inspiration from Pallasmaa in proposing that the worshipping community considers all of its embodied presence as 'haptic', that is, in one way or another, a form of touch. This is, I propose, consistent with, and indeed a demand of, the particular ecclesiology of Christian assembly as identified in the first chapter.

The touching place

O taste and see that the Lord is good. *Psalm 34:8*

To the lost Christ shows his face,
To the unloved he gives his embrace.
To those who cry in pain or disgrace,
Christ makes for himself a touching place.[181]

This popular contemporary hymn "The Touching Place" celebrates the incarnational theology described above. The presence and purpose of God is

---

180 J.J.Gibson, The Senses Considered as Perceptual Systems, (Westport, Conn.: Greenwood Press, 1983). As noted by Pallasmaa.

181 John Bell and Graham Maule, The Touching Place, © Iona Community, in Common Ground (Edinburgh: St Andrews Press, 1998) and in many other collections.

understood as a reaching into the physical world, both in the historic events of Christ's earthly ministry and in his ongoing presence 'in all things' and 'through all things', the continuing work of creation's redemption. It is in the glorious and harsh realities of the physical world that God is present, and into which God calls his people. The worshipping community has, in this sense, been 'touched into being' as it has responded to the glorious and harsh realities of the Word made flesh. It is only in touching the world that we are present to it, as God is present to it in Christ. When the worshipping community gathers, therefore, its quest for connectedness with God, with the world and with one other will be satisfied in so far as the experience is haptic (from the Greek *haptesthai* meaning of, or related to, touch).

Pallasmaa's architectural vision is founded the premise that all of the senses are extensions of the tactile sense. There is, he suggests, ample anthropological and physiological evidence for the primacy of the haptic realm, the perceptual mode that integrates whole-body experience:

> All the senses, including vision, are extensions of the tactile sense; the senses are specialisations of skin tissue, and all sensory experiences are modes of touching and thus related to tactility. Our contact with the world takes place at the boundary line of the self through specialised parts of our enveloping membrane....[The skin] is the oldest and the most sensitive of our organs, our first medium of communication, and our most efficient protector ... Even the transparent cornea of the eye is overlain by a layer of modified skin ... Touch is the parent of our eyes, ears, nose, and mouth. It is the sense which became differentiated into the others, a fact that seems to be recognised in the age-old evaluation of touch as "the mother of

the senses". Touch is the sensory mode that integrates our experience of the world with that of ourselves. Even visual perceptions are fused and integrated into the haptic continuum of the self; my body remembers who I am and where I am located in the world.[182]

For the American architect Kahn too, to see is "only to touch more accurately"[183]. If, as George MacLeod puts it, "matter matters", then the colour, sound, scent, weight, texture and temperature of matter insist on bodily interaction that is haptic in the widest terms. Touch is not simply the business of what occurs at the surface of the skin, but also involves the tactile-muscular and tactile-kinaesthetic senses, which are both central to whole-body experience and are inherently spatial. According to Torevell[184], anthropological research demonstrates that collective sensory experience, like olfaction, is important for collectivity and unity. The burning of incense during liturgies, for example, makes it impossible to resist being a participant in the 'fellow-feeling' of the event, as well as providing a symbolic representation of what is invisible.

The environmental arrangements of the worship space impose profound theological influences upon the worshipper's relationship with space and time, as these dimensions are shaped in ways that remind the community of its human potential and its divine inheritance. If the community is to learn to touch the world incarnationally as it acknowledges whole-body experience, and if the sanctity of its environment is located in the embodied interactions of assembled faithful, as explored in Chapter One, then ritual practice and forms must explicitly promote these commitments.

---

182 Juhani Pallasmaa, The Eyes of the Skin, pp.9-10.

183 Louis Khan quoted in Lobell, Between Silence and Light, p.8.

184 D.Torevell, Losing The Sacred (Edinburgh: T&T Clark, 2000), p.194.

Ritual as embodied interaction in pursuit of the sacred

In his belief that ritual is the primary means by which people make the transition from the profane to the sacred world and experience group identity, Durkheim stated clearly that the process is dependent on the group dynamic of assembled participants: "...rites are ways of acting that are born only in the midst of assembled groups whose purpose is to evoke, maintain, or recreate certain mental states of those groups"[185]. In his review of ritual theory, Torevell describes how anthropological perspectives have identified performance as the dynamic which characterises rituals as mutual, public and collective acts which are always enacted through the physical actions of bodies:

> ...ritual is never a precisional or analytical form of cognitive communication, but works by appealing primarily to the sensual and fleshly bodies, emotions and feelings of the participants. One might term, therefore,....this form of communication "bodily knowing". "Bodily knowing" is a kind of knowing that is felt by the body before, after or alongside the understanding of the mind.[186]

This embodied and affective kind of ritual has, argues Tom Driver[187], been a casualty of the Enlightenment perspective which would consider it primitive in the face of reason. Within the Church, he says, liberal theology has sided with this bias, whilst the reformed tradition has de-emphasised ritual as a function of idolatry, leaving interest in ritual in the hands of conservative forces. In an appeal for the recovery of purposeful and nourishing collective

185 E.Durkheim, Elementary Forms of Religious Life (London: The Free Press, 1995), p.9.
186 D.Torevell, Losing The Sacred, p.32.
187 T.Driver, The Magic of Ritual (San Francisco: Harper, 1991).

ritual (in society generally, but especially within the worship of the church), Driver describes the eucharist as the embodiment of a "liberation ritual". If the message of the gospel is liberation, then the ritual sacrament is the "performance of a freedom", and this, he says, implies freedom of form, and creativity in finding "the means to laugh, cry, play and shockingly truth-tell their way into the world-altering liberty of Christ's presence."[188] Developing Durkheim's group dynamic of "collective effervescence", Driver argues that affective and transforming ritual relies on "mutual presence", whereby being equally present to one's neighbour makes the event sacred in evoking God's presence:

> Jesus" saying that the second of the commandments is like the first, equating love of God with love of neighbour, suggests that in a Christian sacrament the way of God's becoming present to us, and allowing God to be present in return, is for one human being to become radically present to another. The mysterious one who is sacramentally present in worship is not one but two – both the neighbour and God. The experience of such mutual presence is the experience of blessed freedom, a spirit radically opposed to the authoritarianism of the principalities and powers that rule the world in the present age.[189]

Driver's language is arguably extreme, in so far as it imbues the mutuality of participants with a quality that equates with the divine presence, but of importance here is the dependence of meaningful ritual event upon interaction that can only ever be bodily. Northcott argues that the loss of such embodied and mutual ritual is "the principal feature of the corrosive

---

188 Ibid, p.202.

189 Ibid, p.211.

effect of modernity on the Christian churches of northern Europe"[190]. Given that a recovery of ritual is under way in the plethora of 'new-age' religious and para-religious movements in modern societies, the Christian churches have made the mistake of reforming their liturgies by means of "textual archaeology":

> Not enough attention has been paid to the significance and function of ritual, collective performance and celebration as the means of legitimating and making real the spiritual quest of Christians..... Christian ritual needs to be reconstructed in such a way as to re-engage with the cosmic and the natural, with the seasons and the passage of time, with matter and spirit, the psychological, the political and the social, realising the ritual power of Christian ceremony to transform human life in the context of modernity.[191]

The concluding paragraphs will consider some spatial implications for the worshipping community which aspires to whole-body, ritual use of space.

The gathering place

> ...in our reformed religion, it should seem vain to make a parish church larger, than that all who are present can both hear and see. The Romanists, indeed, may build larger churches; it is enough if they hear the murmur of the Mass, and see the elevation of the Host, but ours are to be fitted for Auditories..... it may be thought

190 Michael Northcott, New Age Rites: The Recovery of Ritual, in The Way, (London: July 1993), p.189.

191Ibid, p.197.

reasonable that a new church should be at least 60 feet broad and 90 feet long... these proportions may be varied, but to build more room, than that every person may conveniently hear and see, is to create noise and confusion.

Sir Christopher Wren[192], instructions for rebuilding after The Great Fire of London

The New Testament has much to say about the calling of God's holy people; not much to say about altar design. *Richard Giles[193]*

In understanding the nature of a chapel, I said first you have a sanctuary, and the sanctuary is for those who want to kneel. Around the sanctuary is an ambulatory, and the ambulatory is for those who are not sure, but who want to be near. Outside is a court for those who want to feel the presence of the chapel. And the court has a wall. Those who pass the wall can just wink at it. *Louis Kahn[194]*

This particular fragment of Louis Kahn's lyricism is attractive because it is a view of ecclesiastical space by a renowned architectural theorist which is primarily experiential. The image of concentric circles is both generous and gentle in its desire to accommodate and include those with diverse adherence. Most importantly, it is about degrees of participation, about inclusion, and about bodily presence to the space and to others.

In my opening chapter I set out to show that the historic prevalence for 'monumentalism' in Christian sacred space is untenable in the face of the

192 Sir Christopher Wren, quoted in M.S.Briggs, Puritan Architecture and its Future (London: Butterworth Press, 1946), p.30.

193 Richard Giles, Creating Uncommon Worship (Norwich: Canterbury Press, 2004), p.56.

194 Louis Khan, quoted in Lobell, Between Silence and Light, p.47.

biblical emphasis on the gathered community, or assembly. Given that the assembly has, by definition, to be present to a given physical place, I have argued that bodily interaction with the worship environment and between its occupants is the locus of sanctity, since it is affective bodily experience that allows for both an incarnational theology and its associated mutuality. Contemporary (Anglican) liturgical reformer Richard Giles follows up his introduction to the architectural reordering of church buildings (referred to in Chapter One) with a development of a New Testament theology of liturgical practice[195]. As Dean of Philidelphia Cathedral, Giles describes the outcomes of reshaping the internal liturgical space and practice as a direct response to the theology of 'every member ministry'. Giles' principle inspiration is the description of the community of faith in 1 Peter 2:5 & 9:

> ...like living stones, let yourselves be built into a spiritual house, to be a holy priesthood, to offer spiritual sacrifices acceptable to God through Jesus Christ.....you are a chosen race, a royal priesthood, a holy nation, God's own people, in order that you may proclaim the mighty acts of him who called you out of darkness into his marvellous light.

For Giles, this key description of the gathered community as a 'priesthood' must be given expression in the eucharist - the definitive liturgical act from the earliest era of the church. For Giles, the fact that this key text is written in the plural mode, addressed to the whole community, has obvious implications for the physical arrangement of the gathering. Full bodily participation in the liturgical action by the whole people of God has been, says Giles, the norm at the beginning, and at the various periods of

---

195 Giles, Creating Uncommon Worship (Norwich: Canterbury Press, 2004)

reformation and renewal in Christian history. The principal means by which consecutive hierarchies have sought to disenfranchise the priesthood of all the faithful has been to deprive them of the space necessary for anything other than propositional consent:

> In the typical interior derived from the traditional gothic floor plan of nave and chancel, the impossibility of moving around, or of moving furniture, or of deviating from the given norm of a rigid seating configuration facing in one direction, is all part of the conspiracy to deprive the people of God of their liturgical birthright.[196]

Lack of explorable space itself is, for Giles, an expression of authoritarianism on the part of church hierarchies which implicitly reject shared priesthood.

This is most clearly expressed in the normative provision of the fixed pews that have almost universally filled worship spaces in the church architecture of recent centuries. Although the pew-bound worshipper is able to be present through visual and auditory experience (albeit within the limitations of fixed position), it is principally as a passive spectator or attendee. The arrangement of seating (fixed pews or chairs) in mono-directional rows facing a separate sanctuary or altar operates to put the participants into a clear dialectic of provider (usually sacerdotal or kerygmatic clergy) and consumer. Further, this configuration serves to limit the possibility of corporate experience. A view comprising the backs of heads provides little or no opportunity to encounter the presence and experience of others visually, aurally or physically. The result is inevitably to nurture a culture of individualism. As Kavanagh puts it:

---

196 Ibid, p.54.

Pews, which entered liturgical space only recently, nail the assembly down, proclaiming that the liturgy is not a common action but a preachment perpetrated upon the seated, an ecclesiastical opera done by virtuosi for a paying audience. Pews distance the congregation, disenfranchise the faithful, and rend the assembly.[197]

Although Giles' theological rationale is convincing, I would argue that he should offer more than his passing appeal to embodied experience. Although, as he says, the internal arrangements of the worship space need to identify and communicate clearly the holy, priestly calling of the assembly, he pays little attention to the importance of whole-body experience in this participation. Three pages are devoted to "awakening the senses" (explaining that things should look and smell appealing), whereas we have seen that not only is psychophysical perception the basis of locating the self in time and space, but that human sciences and theologies of the body imply that whole-body experience will principally govern the formative affectivity of experience in any given environment and at any given moment.

It is when the participant's whole-body experience allows him or her to 'feel' the interdependent mutuality of the Body of Christ that appropriate allegiances and an incarnational spirituality will be nurtured. The arrangement of the faithful in pews, therefore, is not merely a theological question to be debated by traditionalists and modernisers, or the subject of heritage-preservation legislation, but a central factor in the articulation of the worshipping community's spirituality. Architecturally, this coincides with the "theatrical strategies of allurement" identified by Lindsay Jones (referred to in Chapter One) in his description of sacred architecture as "ritual event":

197A.Kavanagh, Elements of Rite, (Collegeville, MN: Fortress Press, 1990), p.21. Cited by Giles, ibid, p.54.

If allurement... depends on transforming initially uninterested spectators into committed 'players' then fixed amphitheatric arrangements pose a special challenge.... such stationary audience-and-stage configurations are very prone to engender lassitude and passivity instead of active involvement. Spoilsports abound in such arrangements and are often allowed to remain largely indifferent to the proceedings being staged in front of them.[198]

In concluding this chapter, my contention is that it is insufficient for those who form the worshipping community to learn about their status as embodied members of the corporate priesthood, or to merely assent to that proposition. It is the gathered and physical presence of the assembly that makes Christian space sacred. Participants can only be meaningfully present (thereby making the space sacred) insofar as they are enabled to be in a haptic relationship with the located assembly. Those who arrange environments for worship, therefore, must not only account for, but also pursue, forms that manifest spatial expressions of embodied community.

---

198 Lindsay Jones, The Hermeneutics of Sacred Architecture, Vol.2 (Cambridge MA: Harvard University Press, 2000), p.194.

Concluding Remarks

This study began with the proposition that Western Christian worshipping communities have found it hard to resist becoming identified principally as custodians of buildings. This cultural perception reflects the Church's own understanding of sacred space, which, despite the theological correctives offered by various reform movements, has tended to make 'monumentalism' normative. In exploring why this should be the case, I have argued that appeals to the biblical models of God amidst his dynamic people and of Christ present in the 'new temple' of his assembled body of believers have faltered in the face of the practical realities of needing to use physical meeting space. It is not possible to gather the community without being present to a physical location. However, the resulting environments are typically characterised either by attempts to provide suitable accommodation for the divine presence (monuments), or to provide forms that are utilitarian in providing adequate accommodation for the faithful.

The model of ritual-architectural event suggests that experience of the sacred is located in the interaction of worshippers and their environment, and I have argued, therefore, that it is to the nature of this interaction that we must look. Human interaction with the physical environment demands a commitment to the importance of the human body. Despite the complex story of the Christian church's ambivalence towards the body, I have concluded that anything less than an embodied theology will promote worship practice that dislocates the community from attainable felt response.

I have explored something of the physical and psycho-physical nature of embodied interaction with the environment (particularly of visual and auditory experience) and have attempted to demonstrate that these have profound implications for the worshipping community. Worship spaces should not be thought of as neutral, immovable accidents of history or expensive but necessary evils. The embodied community of Christ must acknowledge an inevitable bodily relationship with its chosen environment and nurture an awareness of its critical influence upon the community's sense of the sacred and of its own presence in the world.

> We declare to you what was from the beginning, what we have heard, what we have seen with our eyes, what we have looked at and touched with our hands, concerning the word of life - this life was revealed, and we have seen it and testify to it, and declare to you the eternal life that was with the Father and was revealed to us - we declare to you what we have seen and heard so that you also may have fellowship with us; and truly our fellowship is with the Father and with his Son Jesus Christ. We are writing these things so that our joy may be complete. *1 John 1:1-4*

Bibliography

Ackerman, Diane A Natural History of the Senses (London: Phoenix, 1996).

Alexander, C et.al. A Pattern Language (New York: Oxford University Press, 1977).

Barrett, C.K. The Gospel According to St John (London: SPCK, 1978).

Barclay, William The Gospel of John, Vol.2 (Edinburgh: St Andrew Press, 1973).

Bell, Cindy Community Choirs, (in International Journal of Research in Choral Singing 2(1), 2004).

Bell, John, L. The Singing Thing (Glasgow: Wild Goose Publications, 2000).

Berger, Peter The Homeless Mind : modernization and consciousness (Hammondsworth: Penguin, 1974).

Berlin, Brent & **Kay**, Paul

  Basic Colour Terms; their universality and evolution (Berkeley: University of California Press, 1969).

Birren, Faber Light, Colour and Environment (New York: Van Nostrand Reinhold, 1982).

Briggs, M.S. Puritan Architecture and its Future (London: Butterworth Press, 1946).

Brueggemann, W.   Genesis: in The Bible Commentary for Teaching
and Preaching (Atlanta: John Knox Press, 1982).

Brook, Peter   The Empty Space (London: Penguin, 1968).

Brown, Peter   The Body and Society (London: Faber and Faber,
1989).

Boyce, P.R.   Illuminance, Visual Performance and Preference
(in Lighting Research and Technology, 5, 1973).

Boyce, P.R.   Human Factors in Lighting (London: Applied
Science Publishers, 1981).

Coakley, Sarah (ed.)   Religion and the Body (Cambridge: Cambridge
University Press, 1997).

Davis, Charles   Body as Spirit: the nature of religious feeling
(London: Hodder, 1976).

Debuyst, Frederic   Modern Architecture and Christian Celebration
(London: Lutterworth, 1968).

Descartes, R.   Selected Philosophical Writings (Cambridge:
Cambridge University Press, 1988).

De Waal, Esther   A Life Giving Way: a commentary on the Rule of St
Benedict (London: Chapman, 1995).

De Waal, Esther   The Celtic Vision: selected and edited from the
Carmina Gadelica (London: DLT, 1988).

Dreher, B. & **Robinson,** S. (ed)

Vision and Visual Dysfunction/Vol 3 (Houndmills: Macmillan Press, 1991).

Driver, T.   The Magic of Ritual (San Francisco: Harper, 1991).

Durkheim, E.   Elementary Forms of Religious Life (London: The Free Press, 1995).

Edwards, L. & **Torcellini,** P.

A Literature Review of the Effects of Natural Light on Building Occupants (Colorado: National Renewable Energy Laboratory, TP-550-30769, July 2002).

Eliade, Mircea   Patterns in Comparative Religion (London: Sheed and Ward, 1958).

Eisenstein, Elizabeth   The Printing Press an an Agent of Change (Cambridge: Cambridge University Press, 1979).

Ferguson, Ronald   George MacLeod, founder of the Iona Community (London: Collins, 1990).

Gibson, J.J.   The Senses Considered as Perceptual Systems, (Westport, CN: Greenwood Press, 1983).

Giles, Richard   Re-Pitching The Tent (Norwich: Canterbury Press, 1996).

Giles, Richard   Creating Uncommon Worship (Norwich: Canterbury Press, 2004).

Gorringe, Timothy   The Education of Desire (London: SCM, 2001).

Gregory, Richard   The Intelligent Eye (London: Weidenfeld and Nicolson, 1970).

Gregory, Richard   Eye and Brain: the psychology of seeing (Oxford: Oxford University Press, 1997).

Gropius, Walter   The Scope of Total Architecture (New York: Collier Books, 1970/1943).

Hammond, Peter (ed)   Towards a Church Architecture (London: Architectural Press, 1962).

Handel, Stephen   Listening: An Introduction to the Perception of Auditory Events (Cambridge, Mass: MIT Press, 1989).

Harrison, B.W.   The Power of Anger in the Work of Love: Christian ethics for women and other strangers, (in Union Seminary Quarterly Review 36 Supp.(1981).

Hertzberger, Herman   Lessons for Students in Architecture (Amsterdam: Uitgeverij, 1991).

Humphrey, Nicholas   A History of the Mind (London: Chatto & Windus, 1992).

Isherwood, Lisa & **Stuart,** Elizabeth

     Introducing Body Theology (Sheffield: Sheffield Acad Press, 1998).

Jones, Lindsay	The Hermeneutics of Sacred Architecture, Volumes 1& 2 (Cambridge MA: Harvard University Press, 2000).
Kavanagh, A.	Elements of Rite (Collegeville, MN: Fortress Press, 1990).
Kavanagh, Donncha	Ocularcentrism and its Others (in Organisation Studies 25(3), London: Sage Publications, 2004).
Laing, Ronald D.	The Politics of Experience (New York: Pantheon Books, 1967).
Laing, Ronald D.	The Divided Self (Harmondsworth/Penguin, 1965).
Lam, William, C.	Perception and Lighting as Formgivers for Architecture (New York: McGraw-Hill, 1977).
Liberman, Jacob	Light: Medicine of the Future (Santa Fe: Bear & Co Publishing, 1991).
Lobell, John	Between Silence and Light: spirit in the architecture of Louis I. Kahn, (Boston: Shaubhala, 1985).
Lockyer, Herbert	All The Music of the Bible (Peabody Mass: Hendrickson Publishers Inc, 2004).
Lossky, Vladimir	The Mystical Theology of the Eastern Church (Cambridge: James Clarke, 1957).
Madaule, Paul	Listening and Singing (in NATS Journal of Singing: Jacksonville FL May/June 2001).
Maconie, Robin	The Science of Music (Oxford: Clarendon Press, 1997).

Mahnke, Frank   Colour, Environment and Human Response
                        (New York: Van Nostrand Reinhold, 1996).

Mellor, Philip & **Shilling,** Chris
                        Reforming the Body: religion, community and
                        modernity (London: Sage, 1997).

Michel, Lou   Light: The Shape of Space (New York: Van
                        Nostrand Reinhold, 1996).

Miles, Margaret   Carnal knowing : female nakedness and religious
                        meaning in the Christian west (Tunbridge Wells :
                        Burns & Oates, 1992).

Moore, B.C.J.   An introduction to the psychology of hearing
                        (San Diego/London: Academic Press, 1997).

Nelson, James. B   Body Theology (Westminster, 1992).

Nelson, James. B   Embodiment (London: SPCK, 1979).

Newell, J. Philip   in Coracle: Journal of the Iona Community
                        (October 2004).

Newell, J. Philip   Echo of the Soul (Canterbury: Morehouse/
                        Canterbury Press, 2000).

Northcott, M.   New Age Rites: The Recovery of Ritual, (in The
                        Way, London: July 1993).

Ong, Walter   The Presence of the Word (New Haven: Yale
                        University Press, 1967).

Ong, Walter   Orality and Literacy (London: Methuen, 1982).

Ott, J.N.   Effects of wavelengths of light on physiological functions of plants and animals, (in Illuminating Engineer Society, 1967).

Ott, J.N.   Colour and Light: their effects on plants, animals and people, (in International Journal of Biosocial Research, 7, 1985).

Ott, J.N.   Light, Radiation and You (Greenwich, CT: Devin-Adair Publishers, 1982,1990).

Pallassmaa, Juhani   The Eyes of the Skin: architecture and the senses, (Chichester: Wiley, 2005).

Prokes, Mary T.   Toward a Theology of the Body (Edinburgh: T&T Clark, 1996).

Radocy, R.E. & **Boyle,** J.D.

                    Psychological Foundations of Musical Behaviour (Illinois: Thomas, 2003).

Robinson, J.A.T.   Liturgy Coming To Life (London: Mowbray, 1960).

Robinson, J.A.T.   The Body: a study in Pauline theology (London: SCM, 1952).

Saliers, D. & **Saliers,** E.   A Song To Sing, A Life To Live (San Francisco: Jossey-Bass, 2005).

Savides, T.J., **Messin,** S.,**Senger,** C., **Kripke,** D.

                    Natural light exposure of young adults (in Physiology and Behavior, 38(4), Oct 1986).

Sheldrake, Philip   <u>Spaces for the Sacred: place, memory and identity</u> (London: SCM, 2001).

Schnackenburg, R.   <u>The Gospel According to St John</u> (London: Burns and Oates, 1968).

Tanizaki, Junichirō   <u>In Praise of Shadows</u> (London: Vintage, 2001).

Tomatis, Alfred   <u>The Ear and Language</u> (Norval: Moulin Publishing, 1996).

Tomatis, Alfred   <u>The Conscious Ear</u> (Barrytown: Station Hill Press, 1991).

Torevell, D.   <u>Losing The Sacred</u> (Edinburgh: T&T Clark, 2000).

Turner, Harold   <u>From Temple To Meeting House: the phenomenology and theology of places of worship</u> (The Hague: Mouton, 1979).

Van der Leeuw, G.   <u>Religion in Essence and Manifestation: a study in phenomenology</u> trans. J.E.Turner, 2 vols. (Glos, Mass.: Peter Smith, 1967).

Verney, Thomas   <u>The Secret Life of the Unborn Child</u> (New York: Dell, 1981).

Von Rad, Gerhard   <u>Genesis</u> (London: SCM, 1961).

Watson, Aaron   Hearing Again the Sound of the Neolithic (in <u>British Archaeology</u>, 23, April 1997).

Westermann, Claus   <u>Genesis 1-11 : a continental commentary</u> (Minneapolis:Fortress Press, 1994).

Wigram, Anthony   The Effects of Vibroacoustic Therapy on Clinical and Non-Clinical Populations, (Unpublished PhD Research Thesis, St George's Hospital, London University).